The History of U.S. Immigration

Coming to America

Ann Byers

Enslow Publishers, Inc.
40 Industrial Road
Box 398
Berkeley Heights, NJ 07922
USA
　　　http://www.enslow.com

Library of Congress Cataloging-in-Publication Data:

Byers, Ann.
    The history of U.S. immigration : coming to America / Ann Byers.
      p. cm. — (The American saga)
    Includes bibliographical references and index.
    ISBN 0-7660-2574-8
    1. United States—Emigration and immigration—History—Juvenile literature. 2. Immigrants—United States—History—Juvenile literature.
    I. Title. II. Series.
    JV6450B87 2006
    304.8'73—dc22

                    2005034653

Printed in the United States of America

10 9 8 7 6 5 4 3 2 1

To Our Readers:
We have done our best to make sure all Internet addresses in this book were active and appropriate when we went to press. However, the author and the publisher have no control over and assume no liability for the material available on those Internet sites or on other Web sites they may link to. Any comments or suggestions can be sent by e-mail to comments@enslow.com or to the address on the back cover.

Illustration Credits: ©Andrew Holbrooke/The Image Works, p. 10; ©Corel Corporation, pp. 1 (center), 62, 70, 72, 93; Getty Images, pp. 43, 101, 104; ©Jack Kurtz/The Image Works, p. 110; The Library of Congress, pp. 1 (left and right), 18, 29, 30, 41, 46, 48, 51, 53, 74, 80, 84, 94, 108; ©Mary Evans Picture Library/The Image Works, p. 76; National Archives and Records Administration, pp. 4, 83; ©North Wind/North Wind Picture Archives, pp. 35, 54; ©Topham/The Image Works, p. 66; U.S. Coast Guard, p. 97.

Cover Illustration: Photodisc: Government and Social Issues/Getty Images (large image); U.S. Coast Guard (inset).

Contents

This Czech woman weeps as she salutes Adolf Hitler after the Nazis invaded her region of Sudetenland in 1938. Some Jews escaped the German onslaught by immigrating to other countries.

Escape From Germany

Kurt Burger had to leave. Life in Germany had become unbearable. It started six years before, when the Nazis came to power. That was when he lost his job. He had held the job for twenty-eight years. Since the Nazi government had started persecuting Jews, no one would hire him or his wife, Charlotte. (Charlotte Burger had a Jewish ancestor.) Their savings had dwindled to almost nothing.

The harsh treatment had turned violent. Kurt feared for himself, his wife, and their six-year-old son, Ralph. So, they decided to leave the Germany they loved.

Actually leaving, however, was not easy. In 1939, very few countries were accepting refugees from Nazi Germany. The Burgers were more fortunate than many others, however. Charlotte Burger had an uncle who lived in America. The United States was not receiving refugees either, but her uncle offered to sponsor the family in the United States. That meant that he would be responsible for them. Uncle Dick would help them find jobs. He would pay their bills until they could pay the bills themselves.

With Uncle Dick's signed promise in hand, Kurt Burger went to the office of the U.S. consul in Berlin. In that city alone, thousands of people were trying to get visas to go to America. Thousands more in dozens of other cities were also attempting to flee. With great difficulty, Kurt Burger was able to persuade the American consul to grant visas to the Burger family. They had permission to go to the United States! But they had to figure out how to get there.

At that time, the only way for a family to make such a move was by sea. But the Nazi government was not allowing passenger boats to leave from Germany. Desperate, the family traveled four hundred miles to the Dutch city of Rotterdam. By then—late September 1939—the German army was on the Dutch border, ready to invade the Netherlands. With only hours to spare, the Burgers managed to board a Dutch ship.

The Burgers had very little with which to start their new life. All they owned now was $7.50 and what they could cram into seven boxes. But they had hope. That hope exploded into grateful tears when the boat glided past the Statue of Liberty near New York City. Kurt Burger knew about Emma Lazarus's poem engraved on the statue's base. It welcomed the "tired," the "poor," the "homeless," the people "yearning to breathe free." The Burger family fit that description. The poem called the statue the "Mother of Exiles." The Burgers were certainly exiles, no longer welcome in the land of their birth.

Uncle Dick brought them to his home in Casper, Wyoming. Even with help, however, starting over was not easy. The Burgers did not speak English. The only work Kurt could find was as a clerk in a store. His wife got a job as a maid in a hotel. They worked hard and saved what they could.

After many months, they did not need Uncle Dick's help anymore. They bought a small grocery store. Tending the store for almost fifteen hours a day, they were soon able to buy their own home. Eventually, the Burgers bought four more houses that they rented to others. Charlotte Burger gave birth to a daughter three years after their arrival.

The Burgers used their savings to bring some of their relatives to the United States. They wanted others in their family to share in the freedom and bounty they had found in America. Meanwhile, from 1930 to 1945, the Nazis killed over 6 million Jews in Europe.

Thirty years after leaving Germany, Burger was still grateful for all America had given him. In a letter to his son, he wrote, "Could I repay this country for giving me and my family refuge and the salvation from an unspeakable end?"[1] He had been a good neighbor and citizen. He had planted trees, paid his taxes, and contributed to his city. He had raised two children who were also good Americans. Could that ever be thanks enough for all America had done for him? It had saved him from certain death. It had given him the opportunity to restore the peace and prosperity he had once enjoyed in Germany.

Burger and his family gave much to their new country. They brought with them to Casper their strong values of family and community. They worked hard and sacrificed for their children and their future. They felt a responsibility to treat others fairly, to help people in need, and to do what they could to improve themselves and their community.

These gifts they brought to the United States enriched the people of Casper. As the family became

"Could I repay this country for giving me and my family refuge and the salvation from an unspeakable end?"

—Kurt Burger, a Jewish immigrant from Germany

Americanized, the Americans they met became more like them. They adopted some of the attitudes and practices of their once-German neighbors. Just as thousands of immigrants before them and since have done, Kurt and Charlotte Burger wove the tattered threads of their lives into the fabric of America. Like bright shapes in a patchwork quilt, their presence made the nation larger, stronger, and more colorful.

Settling America

Immigration is a two-part move. First, it involves *emigrating*, or moving out of one country; and, second, it involves *immigrating*, or moving into another. Both are drastic actions. Most people think long and hard before taking such serious steps. A number of circumstances can influence their decisions. These circumstances are called pushes and pulls.

A *push* is something that drives people out of a country. It is usually some unpleasant situation. Often it is economic: a depression, a crop failure, or general poverty. Sometimes an economic disaster such as a famine strikes large portions of a country. A large-scale catastrophe can push many people out. A smaller calamity may affect only a few people.

A push can be political. If a ruler mistreats his or her subjects, the people do not want to stay. When the political situation is unstable, citizens may not feel safe. High taxes can drive people away. Drafting citizens into the military is often unpopular. All these things can lead to emigration.

Discrimination may push people out of their native land. When the discrimination becomes outright

Harsh conditions in a country can cause people to emigrate to another nation. These children in Somalia are suffering from starvation.

persecution, victims are often forced to flee. This is what happened to Kurt Burger and his family.

Where emigrants go depends on what country has the strongest pull. A *pull* is something that attracts people to a particular place. Pulls are usually the opposite of pushes. If someone left a country because of no job, he or she would choose to come to a nation that had jobs. If he or she emigrated to escape war, he or she would immigrate to a place at peace.

Like pushes, pulls are frequently economic. People may be lured by the promise of work or the rumor of gold. They may hear that land is cheap. Pulls might be political. Oppressed people immigrate to countries where they can be free. Frequently the draw is a relative who lives in the new land.

Emigrants are not always "pushed" out of their land. They may simply be restless. Or they may leave because of a strong pull. Similarly, immigrants are not necessarily "pulled" to a specific place. A push may be so great that they go to whatever country is available. It may be nearby, it may invite foreigners, or it may be the only country that will accept certain people.

The First Immigrants

No one knows the pushes and the pulls that might have brought the first people to America. No one is even sure from where they emigrated. For decades, scholars thought the earliest Americans came from Asia about 11,500 years ago. They assumed that Alaska was once connected with Siberia in northern Asia. Today, the waters of the Bering Strait separate the two continents. But thousands of years ago, a bridge of land joined them. People could have walked across that bridge. They might have been following herds of animals they hunted for food. After they reached Alaska, the scholars thought, the people kept moving south. Over many centuries, they filled both North America and South America.

Lately, however, scholars have a different theory. They have found bones and other evidence that suggests that people were on the continent a thousand years earlier, about 12,500 years ago. Many scientists today think the first Americans came by sea instead of land. They immigrated across the Pacific Ocean in boats. They may have come from Europe, southern Asia, or Africa. They would have settled along the coast and then moved inland.[1]

However they came, they were the first immigrants to America. Their descendants are sometimes called American Indians, Amerindians, or Native Americans.

Early European Colonists

We do know how and when the next group of immigrants came to America. After Christopher Columbus's arrival in the Caribbean in 1492, several countries attempted to start colonies in what they called the New World—the Caribbean, South America, and North America. The first colonists were not pushed from Europe by any disaster. Rather, they were pulled to America by the possibility of adventure, economic gain, and political glory. They wanted to have colonies so they could claim the territory and its wealth for their nations.

The first country to be successful was Spain.[2] In the early 1500s, Spain brought people to settle the New World. They came mostly to the coast of what are now Mexico and South and Central America. They moved inland and northward. In 1565, Spanish explorers founded the first permanent colony in what would become the United States. Called St. Augustine, it was located in what is now Florida. Using that colony as a base, other immigrants from Spain built forts and missions as far north as present-day North Carolina.

During this period, France was also exploring the New World. After a few short-lived attempts to establish colonies in Florida and the Carolinas, the French sailed north. They settled mainly on the coast and along the rivers of Canada. From there, many moved down the Mississippi River.

Great Britain also eyed the newly discovered continent. For much of the sixteenth century, Britain and Spain fought for dominance in the New World. When the British navy defeated the Spanish Armada in 1588, Britain gained control of the Atlantic Ocean between Europe and America. From that point on, the major colonial activity in North America was British.

The first successful British colony was founded in 1607 in Jamestown, Virginia. It was begun as a trading post. That meant that a trading company, the Virginia Company, owned the land. The company hoped to make money from the land. It needed to discover what products the land held. English merchants could sell those products in Europe. For the plan to work, the trading company needed people to live and work in Jamestown.

But the New World had little pull to attract immigrants. Who would want to brave an eight- to ten-week ocean voyage and unknown dangers with no promise of reward? To attract settlers, the Virginia Company painted glowing pictures of the land. But they still could entice only a few people to come. The settlers endured bitter cold and biting hunger. They were attacked by American Indians, who were angry because the colonists were taking their land.

The Europeans were short on supplies and long on illnesses.

Some settlers survived, however. They learned to grow tobacco, which sold well in Europe. They were allowed to own land. Women immigrated and became their wives. The prospect of a farm, family, and fortune drew many to the New World. They brought with them English laws and government. English government was unique in Europe. In most European countries, kings or emperors reigned. But England, although it had a king, also had a lawmaking body called Parliament. The first immigrants ensured that the country that would become the United States would be a nation governed by democratic principles.

Pilgrims and Puritans

The success of Jamestown encouraged another immigration attempt. A group known as the Pilgrims set up a colony on the coast of present-day Massachusetts, far north of Jamestown. Some of the Pilgrims were part of a separatist religious group who called themselves the "Saints." They wanted to separate from the Church of England. When they heard the exaggerated stories about the glories of America, some of them decided to go there.

The goal of the Saints was neither fortune nor adventure. They were pushed from their native country by lack of religious freedom. And they were pulled to America by its distance from England, by the hope of being completely on their own.

One hundred two Pilgrims set sail on the *Mayflower* in 1620. Although we call them all Pilgrims today, fewer than half were religious Separatists. Many came in hopes of making good money. Others came for adventure. When they reached America's shore, they found themselves miles from where they had been given permission to settle. They named their landing place Plymouth, after a town in Great Britain. Before the pilgrims got off the ship, the leaders wrote a set of laws that they called the Mayflower Compact, or agreement. All the men on board signed it.

The Plymouth settlement sparked interest in immigration among other religious groups. One group, the Puritans, wondered: If the Pilgrims could start a new life across the sea, could they not do the same? They could build a community that followed the reforms they wanted. They called their idea a "city on a hill."[3] They hoped it would shine as an example that people could live well by following the laws of God.

Between 1630 and 1650, twenty thousand Puritans settled in America.[4] They spread out in five colonies: Plymouth, Massachusetts Bay, Connecticut, New Haven, and the Rhode Island and Providence Plantations.

Puritan immigrants based their practices on their understanding of the Bible. They placed a high value on hard work. This has been called the Protestant work ethic. Puritans believed in the dignity of every person. They did not want to separate nobles from commoners. This led to representative government, where everyone had a say. Two institutions that are still important in American life were begun by the Puritans: the town meeting and free public education. The Puritan ways of thinking, working, governing, and living became American principles.

Dutch and Swedish Immigrants

At the same time Puritans were streaming into New England, Dutch people were arriving from the Netherlands. When the Dutch first came, they established three trading posts along the Hudson River. The Dutch called the area New Netherlands. At the beginning, they were interested only in collecting furs. But in the 1620s, they began to turn their trading posts into settlements. The Dutch West India Company gave a huge estate to any Dutchman who would bring fifty people to the new colony. Those who brought colonists were called patroons.

The patroons could usually find people who were willing to immigrate. During the fifteenth and sixteenth centuries, religious wars raged throughout Europe. Protestants fought Catholics. Different sects fought one another. Many people looked for ways to escape these conflicts. Between 1620 and 1650, about eight thousand immigrated to New Netherlands.[5]

They were not all Dutch. A group of people called Walloons also came. They were French-speaking people originally from Belgium. A small group of Jews originally from Portugal also became part of the Dutch colony.

Although small in numbers, the Dutch immigrants made themselves part of America. Their influence is apparent today in the English language. The word *cookie* comes from the Dutch word for *cake*. The doughnut called a *cruller* was named for the Dutch word for *curl*. The Dutch *baas* became *boss* in English. A cabbage salad is *kool sla* in Dutch and *coleslaw* in English. *Sleigh, snoop,* and *stoop* all come from the people of New Netherlands. The term *Yankees,* used of everyone in New England, was probably originally *Jan Kees,* a nickname for a Dutchman.

The Dutch colony had competition. In 1638, a Swedish company started a settlement on the Delaware River. New Sweden, however, was not very big. It never had more than two hundred to three hundred people, both Swedes and Finns.[6] Nor did it last very long.

In 1655, the tiny colony became part of New Netherlands. The people, however, kept the Swedish language and culture alive for a full century. One of the lasting contributions of the early Swedish immigrants was the log cabin. The Swedes were the first to notch the ends of logs and use them to make homes.

Just as the Dutch swallowed up New Sweden, the English took over New Netherlands. The English king, ignoring the Dutch settlements, gave the area along the Hudson to his brother, the duke of York. The Dutch could not fight against the four gunships the duke sent to their settlement of New Amsterdam. They surrendered and the little post was renamed

In this painting by Jean Leon Gerome Ferris, Dutch residents of New Amsterdam plead with their leader Peter Stuyvesant not to open fire on the British.

New York. Thus, in 1664, the entire Atlantic Coast from New England to what is now South Carolina was ruled by Britain.

African Immigrants

Not everyone who came to America came willingly. Thousands were taken from Africa in chains. In 1619, twenty Africans were brought to Jamestown and sold as workers. These first African immigrants may not have been thought of as slaves. They may have been like indentured servants: having to work in exchange for food and housing. The masters did not own indentured servants. They merely owned their service for a certain amount of time. But the Africans did not have contracts. So there was no set time for their service to end. They could be used as servants for life. By 1700, all men and women brought from Africa and their children were considered slaves.

For most of the 1600s, relatively few Africans were in the English settlements. But as smoking remained popular in Europe, the southern colonies that grew tobacco needed more workers. To fill the desire for labor that did not cost anything, the colonists looked to the Africans. From 1619 until the slave trade was outlawed in 1808, perhaps as many as half a million Africans were brought to the English colonies.[7]

Over 80 percent of the Africans in the English colonies lived in the South.[8] In Virginia and Maryland, they worked on the tobacco plantations. In the Carolinas and Georgia, they toiled in the rice fields. The few who lived in the north usually worked on small farms and as household servants.

More European Immigrants

The colonies were profitable for England. So the English set about filling them with people. The king of England gave large tracts of land in America to some of his nobles. Each noble built his own colony.

To fill Maryland, Lord Baltimore brought Catholic immigrants from England and Ireland. He had become a Catholic and saw Catholics in these countries being persecuted. He wanted his colony to be a safe place for them.

The leaders in the Carolinas first recruited immigrants from England, France, and Scotland. In France, the Huguenots, a Protestant sect somewhat like the Puritans, were suffering severe discrimination. They were invited to the Carolinas to grow silkworms.

Of the thirteen original colonies, the one with the greatest variety of people was Pennsylvania. It was that way on purpose. Its founder, William Penn, belonged to a Puritan-like sect called the Quakers (or the Society of Friends). He believed that people of different beliefs should be able to get along together. He looked on Pennsylvania as a "holy experiment," an "example . . . to the nations."[9] It would have freedom for every religion. And it would have citizens of every faith. Its main city, which Penn designed, would be a town of brotherly love. That is what the name *Philadelphia* means.

For his experiment, Penn wrote up an advertisement. He described the territory. He talked about religious liberty. And he offered land to those who would come. Penn visited Germany, the Netherlands, and Wales to recruit settlers. And people responded. They mixed with the Swedes, Finns, and Dutch who were already in the colony.

Thousands of Scotch-Irish came. They were Presbyterians, members of a Protestant group. They had moved from Scotland to northern Ireland to escape persecution from the Anglican Church. Their lot was no better in Ireland, as Catholics discriminated against them there. Penn's promise of freedom from religious persecution enticed them to America.

Large numbers of Germans came also. Some were

from sects very much like the Quakers: Mennonites, Moravians, Dunkards, and Amish. They, too, fled religious intolerance in their homeland. Many settled in a village outside Philadelphia that is still called Germantown. They founded cities with biblical names such as Bethlehem and Nazareth. Their English-speaking neighbors, misunderstanding the German word *Deutsch* (which means *German*), called them "Pennsylvania Dutch."

Pennsylvania was different from the Puritan colonies of New England. The Puritans wanted to found Puritan settlements. They wanted cities and villages where their beliefs were law. They were not tolerant of people with other religious views. They even made rules against groups such as the Quakers. Penn, on the other hand, wanted a place where religion was a personal matter. He wanted all kinds of people to live in harmony and freedom: English, Irish, Scots, Welsh, Germans, Dutch, Swedes, Finns, Catholics, Protestants, Anglicans, Quakers, and Presbyterians. In Pennsylvania, they did just that. This very mixed group of immigrants established in America the principle of religious freedom.

They also formed the best and earliest example of the multicultural patchwork that America would become. At the end of the seventeenth century, New England was largely English, mostly Puritan. Virginia and Maryland were English-speaking colonies, with people from England and Ireland. The Carolinas had a number of Scots, Irish, and French, but they were still primarily English. The Spanish colonies in Florida were almost entirely Spanish. The French settlements in Louisiana and along the Canadian border were predominantly French. Pennsylvania, however, was made up of people from more than eight different nations.

Getting to America

Very few of the immigrants coming to colonial America could pay for the voyage. And no one else would pay unless they could make a profit on the immigrants. This dilemma was solved with two clever institutions: the head-right system and indenture.

Under the head-right system, the governor owned land. He gave sections of that land to a person who brought colonists. The person receiving the land expected the people he brought to work for him. So they were called servants. The person who paid their way to come to America might be called their master. They were not slaves; they served the master until they had worked off the money he had paid to get them to their new home. The governor gave the master a certain number of acres for every male servant he brought and a certain number of acres for each woman and child. The land belonged to the master, not to the servants who worked it. In addition to paying for the colonists to come, the master had to pay rent to the governor for the land. The governor received money every year. The master got land he could farm. And the immigrant got to start a new life.

But the immigrants' new lives were often not as

rosy as they expected. Many colonists came to America as indentured servants. They signed a contract to work for a master for up to seven years. The contracts were torn in two, one half for the master, one for the servant. Tearing the contract indented the edges. The agreements were therefore called indentures, and the workers were called indentured servants.

During the term of service, the master provided everything for the servant: food, clothing, and housing. When the indenture was over, the servant was free. Usually he or she was then given some clothing, a little food, and a small amount of money. Sometimes the servant also received a bit of land, a few tools, and some seed.

The life of an indentured servant was not easy. The work was often physical and hard. Many died before their term was up. Others ran away. If they were caught, more time was added to their length of service. If a female servant became pregnant, she often had years added to her indenture. Those who were given land when they fulfilled their obligations often found that the land was poor. Those who did not get land became tenant farmers on the farms of their former masters. Some were able to work their way up in society; others remained poor. Despite the difficulties, people continued to indenture themselves because it was the only way they could get to America.[10]

Not all poor immigrants came as indentured servants. Some were criminals and other people the king did not want in his realm. A number of Scots and

Irishmen who were captured in wars with England were exiled to America. Spillovers from overcrowded jails were sent. James Oglethorpe began the colony of Georgia with prisoners. They had been arrested because they could not pay their debts.

America's early immigrants were a mixed group: lords and commoners, skilled craftsmen and untrained peasants, learned men and people who could not read, and ministers and lawbreakers. The great hope of America was that it could make all of them better.

New colonists had to communicate with people who did not understand their language. They learned to prepare and eat foods they had never seen. They invented ways to keep warm in the freezing winters, grow corn in rocky soil, and sew animal skins into clothes. They figured out how to govern themselves. These challenges toughened the immigrants. The struggles made them creative, strong, and proud. They transformed them from immigrants into Americans.

Growing America

By the time the United States became a nation in 1776, Americans of European descent numbered more than 2 million.[1] Three generations of children of the first colonists had been born in America. George Washington, who would become the first U.S. president, was the great-grandson of an immigrant from England. The new country was producing its own "native" people.

And immigrants were still coming. They were arriving at a slower rate, however. From 1775 until 1815, immigration dropped dramatically. During those forty years, wars raged both in Europe and in America. People had difficulty leaving Europe. Ships on the seas were not safe from warring gunboats. And battle weary America was not attractive to people who were tired of wars. Yet still some came. Between 1775 and 1815, about two hundred and fifty thousand Europeans immigrated to the United States.[2]

Pushes and Pulls

By 1820, America had recovered from major wars. The American Revolution and the War of 1812 with the British were both over. The United States was becoming strong. In Europe, however, conditions had become difficult. Internal strife rocked nearly every European nation. Where revolts were crushed, harsh governments often burdened the people. They taxed them heavily. They forced them to serve in their armies and navies. Many Europeans saw America as an escape from political upheaval and oppression.

At the same time, a kind of revolution overtook the farms of Europe. New technologies allowed farmers to produce more and better crops. This meant that people ate better and lived longer. Improvements in medical science also enabled them to live longer. All this led to overpopulation. Between 1790 and 1830, Europe's population doubled.[3] Unlike America, Europe had little unsettled land to which its population could expand. Eventually there was too little land for all the people.

Many of the landless people moved into cities. Beginning in England at the end of the eighteenth century, an industrial revolution transformed Europe. People made goods with machines instead of by hand. Production moved out of homes and into factories. Goods were mass-produced instead of made one at a time. Europe's large population provided plenty of workers for the new industries. But before long there were not enough jobs for the swelling population.

Nor was there enough food. Small family farms could not supply the growing cities with food. Agriculture, like manufacturing, shifted from small-scale to large-scale production. Powerful landlords seized the property of small farmers. They created commercial enterprises. The shift left many farmers without land or work. Many of the landlords sold their products abroad, leaving too little food for their own citizens.

Some of the people of Europe in the 1800s were crowded, poor, hungry, and wretched. In their eyes, America had everything Europe lacked. It had land— acres of good, fertile land. And that land cost a fraction of what much poorer quality land cost in Europe. America had jobs. And those jobs paid twice what the same work paid in Europe. America also had freedom from political strife.

That freedom had allowed industry to blossom in the United States. Blessed with an abundance of natural resources, Americans could produce goods relatively cheaply. They made fabric, clocks, rifles, nails, and dozens of other items. Demand for the manufactured goods, both in the United States and abroad, was constantly growing. Factory owners needed more workers to keep up with the demand.

So they advertised in Europe. Like the colonial recruiters before them, they described a wonderful life in America. Some companies even offered to pay the passage of the immigrants. They would deduct the cost later from the wages they paid them.

Some people were pulled to the United States in a "chain migration." Earlier arrivals wrote letters to relatives in their homelands. They sang the praises of their new country. Sometimes the letters were reprinted in newspapers and read by many. The earlier immigrants encouraged new people to join them in America.

Getting from Europe to America was easy in the mid-nineteenth century. The invention of the steamship had made the journey quick, safe, and relatively inexpensive. Trade across the Atlantic was brisk. Ships coming to America to buy products often had room. The steamship companies, not wanting to waste the space, were happy to fill the boats with people.

The ride on boats made for cargo, not people, was unpleasant. There were no beds and no comforts. Goods and people often crowded the decks. No medicine was available for the many who got sick on the voyage. Still, immigrants were offered cheap tickets for a chance at a better life.

Immigrants from Europe

Between 1820 and 1860, nearly 40 percent of the immigrants were from Ireland.[4] Ireland was a beautiful but miserable place in the 1800s. The English owned most of the land in Ireland. They were the landlords and the Irish were mostly poor farmers. The population had grown so quickly that families were squeezed onto smaller and smaller plots of land. In other countries of Europe, people in this situation found jobs in the cities. However, Ireland had no industry. So there were no jobs for displaced peasants.

To make matters worse, the English landlords

Famous Immigrant
Andrew Carnegie, Industrialist and Philanthropist
(1835–1919)

At age thirteen, Andrew Carnegie immigrated to the United States from Scotland. He had no formal education. His first job was in a cotton mill, making $1.20 per week. Then, beginning as a telegrapher, he worked his way up at the Pennsylvania Railroad Company. He invested his earnings in a railroad business, oil lands, and the iron industry. In 1873, he put all his money into developing steel mills. He became one of the richest men in the world.

When Carnegie was thirty-three, he was earning fifty thousand dollars a year. This was a fortune in 1868. Carnegie said no one should ever earn more than that amount. If he does, he should give the extra away to good causes.

Carnegie followed his own advice. He sold his company for $250 million in 1901 and retired. He spent the rest of his life giving his wealth away. He donated to libraries, colleges, and cultural centers. His money built the Peace Palace for the United Nations (UN) International Court at The Hague, Netherlands. He established foundations that are still giving money to charitable causes.

In the 1800s and early 1900s, many poor Irish people lived in small cottages.

found that Irish beef and butter sold well in England. So instead of growing crops, they decided to raise cattle. They evicted the peasants so they would have more room for the animals. Forced from their homes and their farms, the peasants lived on tiny scraps of land. Around their one-room cottages, they grew potatoes.

Without land or jobs, thousands of Irish looked at America as the land of opportunity. At first, most of the immigrants were young, single men. They were not the poorest of the peasants; the poorest could not afford the move. Many went to Canada to work in the lumber business. From there, they traveled south to better jobs in New England.

Immigration from Ireland jumped dramatically in 1845. In that year, a fungus, or blight, appeared in the potatoes. It destroyed half of the nation's crop, bringing widespread famine. The blight recurred the next year, and the crop was poor for several more years. Between 1845 and 1850 a million Irish died of hunger and disease.[5]

Those who lived could not pay their rent. Thousands were evicted from their homes. Now America was not just the land of opportunity for the young. It was the land of salvation for young and old alike. During the Great Potato Famine, from 1845 to 1848, 1.5 million Irish came to the United States.[6]

These immigrants were different from the Irish who had settled during the Colonial period. Most of the earlier immigrants had been Scotch-Irish. They were Protestants from Northern Ireland. Many were skilled in some trade. They were very much like the English colonists. The newer settlers, however, were poor, and most of them only knew how to farm. Also, instead of being Protestant, they were Catholic.

The next largest immigrant group of the early 1800s also contained farmers. They were Germans, and they made up about a third of the immigrants of this period.[7] As in Ireland, they left their land because of population pressures, economic depression, land seizures, and famine. In the 1820s, a number of Jews immigrated to

Famous Immigrant
Levi Strauss, Tailor
(1829–1902)

Born in Bavaria, Germany, Levi Strauss was the youngest of seven children. At age eighteen, he immigrated to New York. He worked with two of his brothers in a family business, selling cloth and making clothing.

After gold was discovered in California, Strauss moved to San Francisco. He thought he could sell his cloth to the people looking for gold. His plan was to use canvas material to make tents and covers for covered wagons. Instead, he learned that what the prospectors needed was sturdy pants. So he stitched his canvas into pants. Later, he added copper rivets to make the pockets stronger.

He also changed from canvas to a material called serge de Nimes (denim), meaning "dyed with indigo." The material was called *genes* in France. So the pants became known as jeans. But most people called them Levi's. The first pants sold for twenty-two cents. Today, they are made almost exactly the same way as they were in the 1800s.

Levi Strauss became a U.S. citizen in 1853. He gave money to college scholarship funds, orphanages, and other charities. His family still runs the business.

escape anti-Semitism that was building in Germany. A violent political revolution in 1848 caused even more Germans to flee. Some of the Germans who came to America were well-educated professionals. They were teachers, journalists, and musicians. A number of intellectuals, known as the "forty-eighters," entered the United States after the failed 1848 revolution. But most German immigrants were farmers.

Other Europeans also came to America in the early

nineteenth century. Most were from countries in northern and western Europe. Close to a million came from England, Scotland, Wales, Switzerland, the Netherlands, and the Scandinavian nations. At least one hundred twelve thousand immigrated from Canada.[8]

Immigrants from Mexico

While Europeans were braving the Atlantic, eighty thousand people became citizens of the United States without even moving. They lived in land the United States acquired from Mexico.[9]

The unusual immigration began in 1846. The United States had taken over Texas and wanted to buy California and New Mexico. Mexico refused to sell, and the two countries went to war. The United States won, and the war ended with the Treaty of Guadalupe Hidalgo in 1848. The United States paid Mexico $15 million and gained the land that would become California and parts of Arizona, New Mexico, Nevada, Utah, Wyoming, Kansas, and Colorado. Six years later, in the Gadsden Purchase, the United States bought what is today southern Arizona and southern New Mexico for $10 million.

The vast acres of land were sparsely populated, and many non-Mexicans lived there. For years, Spanish- and English-speakers had lived side by side with little problem. But the discovery of gold in California in 1848 changed the ethnic balance. As Anglos streamed west, Mexicans became a minority. Many of the men who came west in the gold rush were greedy and rough. They pushed the Mexican Americans from their mining claims. They settled wherever they wanted and forced Mexican Americans off their own land.

When the railroads came west, more English speakers came with them. They, too, took whatever land they wished. Because the territory was far from the centers of government, law enforcement was lax. In fact, the army, rangers, and other policing agencies often sided with the Anglos. And in court, judges frequently denied the legitimate claims of Mexican Americans. These government officials allowed ethnic prejudice to override their sense of duty.

Losing their land was a huge blow to the Mexican Americans of the Southwest. Their main occupation was cattle ranching, and cattle required large tracts of land. The majority of Mexican Americans were forced to give up their traditional economy and find jobs on the farms and ranches of others. Some went to cities such as Los Angeles and El Paso. By 1870, Mexican Americans made up only 4 percent of the population of the land they once owned.[10]

Immigrants from China

Mexicans were not the only immigrants in the West. At the same time Europeans were coming to the Atlantic states, men from China were arriving on the Pacific coast.

Conditions in China in the 1800s were similar to those in Europe in some ways. The British Opium Wars and other trade conflicts had devastated China's economy. When the government imposed heavy taxes on the peasants, they revolted. A series of mid-century floods wiped out part of the rice crop. Yet, these powerful pushes were not the main forces behind Chinese emigration. The Chinese came to America primarily because of a single, glittering pull.

In 1848, gold was discovered in California. Sailors were the first to bring the news to China. As they traded American manufactured goods for Chinese tea

Chinese immigrants wait to be officially admitted into the United States in a San Francisco customhouse in the 1870s.

and silk, they talked about the gold. Rumors spread quickly that fortunes could be made in the United States. Before long, poor peasants in China were abuzz with stories of a mountain of gold in America. Those stories gave California the Chinese name it still bears: Gold Mountain.

By 1852, twenty-five thousand Chinese had come to California.[11] Thousands more came in the years following. Most did not intend to stay. Their plan was to mine the riches of Gold Mountain and take their treasure back to China. Almost all the immigrants were men. They did not bring their families, for they hoped to return to their villages.

When they arrived in California, they did indeed find gold. But they also found discrimination and hostility. Many of the white miners resented the success of the Chinese. They looked for ways to take their gold from them.

They found a way in an 1852 foreign miner's tax. The state of California imposed a tax of twenty dollars a month on every miner who was not a U.S. citizen. Some of the Asian immigrants had to abandon their mines because they could not pay the tax. Those who could afford the tax were often pushed off their claims by greedy whites. In the rough and lawless West, a number of miners did not hesitate to kill Chinese for their gold.

Forced out of the mines, the Chinese needed to make money. Most had no skills but farming. Very few spoke English. Only the lowest jobs were open to them.

Some worked as laborers in construction. Others became household servants or cooks. Many found jobs in factories, sewing or making boots, shoes, and cigars.

Some made their own business opportunities. They noticed that the miners were dirty and hungry. Perhaps they would be willing to spend some of their gold for clean clothes and decent food. Thus, the Chinese began laundries and restaurants. They also fished the San Francisco and Monterey bays. They opened shops. But most could not make enough money for a ticket back to China. Gold Mountain turned out to be a towering disappointment for them.

Becoming Americans

Most immigrants, however, were not disappointed with America. Many wanted to become citizens. But in a nation formed by people from many countries, who is a citizen? How does a citizen of Germany or France become a citizen of the United States? Congress had answered that question with the Naturalization Act of March 26, 1790.

Naturalization is the process by which a foreign-born person becomes a citizen. The 1790 law set three qualifications for naturalization. First, citizenship was limited to "free white persons." Children of immigrants who were naturalized were also made citizens. Since slaves and indentured servants were not free, they were not eligible. In fact, no Africans or Asians, even if they were free, could be citizens because they were not white. The second requirement was that a person be of "good moral character."

The third qualification was a residency requirement. Before becoming a citizen, a person had to reside, or live, in the United States for two years and in one state for one year. In 1795, the residency requirement was raised to five years in the country and two in the state.

In 1855, a law allowed women who married U.S. citizens to automatically become citizens themselves. In 1870, naturalization was opened to people of African descent.

Whether the nineteenth-century immigrants became naturalized, they were part of the American saga. They peopled the cities of the East and the farms of the Midwest. They established cities, missions, ranches, and farms throughout the West and Southwest. They helped grow the nation from less than 10 million in 1820 to 30 million in 1860.[12] In those forty years, more than 5 million immigrants made their homes in America.[13]

They did more than enlarge the nation. They built the structures that kept it growing.

Building America

The nineteenth century—more specifically the years from 1820 to 1924—has been called the century of immigration. In these hundred years, almost 36 million people came to America. In the first half of that period, until about 1880, the majority came from western Europe, the Scandinavian countries, and China. They came to make a better life for themselves and their families.

Arriving in America

Many of the new immigrants, however, found that living in the United States was not what they had expected. From the moment they set foot on American soil, they were bombarded with one shock after another. They were met at the dock by hundreds of "runners." These were salesmen sent to get the new arrivals' business. The salesmen tried to entice the immigrants to come to work at their factories, stay at their boardinghouses, or buy their wares. Amid the runners were thieves and pickpockets who were also after the immigrants' money.

The majority of immigrants entered the country

through New York Harbor. At first, no one but runners welcomed them. Then, in 1855, the state of New York opened a processing center to bring some order to the chaos on the docks. The state leased an old fort at the southern tip of Manhattan Island. It was called Castle Garden. Here, officials registered the new arrivals. They tried to protect them from the money grabbers and help them get settled.

Some of the newcomers found their way inland to established communities. But many more, especially the Irish, settled in the coastal cities where they entered the United States. By 1850, a third of the populations of New York City and Boston were Irish. Few of the Irish immigrants had enough money to go any farther. They took whatever job was available at whatever pay. They began on the lowest rung of the employment ladder. They cleaned streets, unloaded ships, and swept stables. The men seldom earned enough to pay for the rent on their squalid rooms, so women went to work as well. The women usually washed the clothes and cleaned the houses of the rich.

Building the Transportation System

To better their lot, some Irish began to move away from the cities. Many, especially the single men, joined construction crews. These crews were building the transportation systems for the young nation. The growing U.S. population was moving westward, and it needed roads to travel on. Immigrant labor cleared the

The Irish started holding St. Patrick's Day parades in New York City in 1762. This mother and daughter watch the parade in 1953.

land, made the roads, and built the bridges that took people west.

The people in the interior of the country needed to stay connected to the coastal cities. They purchased supplies in the East and sold their produce there. They could use rivers to transport goods and supplies, but they had to have canals to connect one river to another. By about 1850, almost five thousand miles of canals were constructed.[1] It was immigrant labor that dug the massive waterways. The Erie Canal probably could not have been built without the work of three thousand Irishmen.[2]

Canals eventually gave way to an even faster method of transportation. Railroads began rapidly snaking their way across the continent. In 1830, the United States had only twenty-three miles of track. In the next ten years, 2,808 miles were laid. By 1860, 30,626 miles of railroad lines laced the Midwest and crossed the Mississippi River.[3] Those lines were laid by immigrants.

In the East, much of the track was laid by the Irish. In the West, the railroads were built largely by the Chinese. Transportation companies had decided to build a railroad line that would span the continent, from the Atlantic to the Pacific. The Union Pacific Railroad line would begin in the East and build west. The Central Pacific would start in California and head east. Somewhere in the middle, the two lines would meet.

In 1864, construction began on the Central Pacific. When building crews reached the rugged Sierra Nevadas, the work grew harder. Hundreds of laborers left their jobs, hoping to strike it rich in the gold mines. That left the railroad short on workers. One of Central Pacific's owners, Charles Crocker, decided to fill the spots with Chinese workers.

The leader of the construction crew did not think the Chinese could do a good job. The work was grueling, and the Asian immigrants were small and thin. How could the frail-looking men dig through the granite mountains? Could they haul wheelbarrows of rock and dirt up and down the steep slopes? Crocker convinced him to give them a try. He hired fifty Chinese.

The new employees surprised everyone. They worked twelve-hour days in drenching rain, scorching

Immigrants worked on building the railroads during the nineteenth century. These workers are building a railroad bridge over a river in Salt Lake City, Utah.

sun, and blinding snow. They kept their camps neat, did not fight, and seldom complained. Central Pacific's president was very pleased with his Chinese workforce. Within two years, he had replaced most of his other men with twelve thousand Chinese. They made up 90 percent of his entire construction crew.[4]

The immigrant construction crews worked hard. Building roads, digging canals, and laying track were grueling and dangerous tasks. Hillsides had to be leveled with dynamite. Tunnels had to be drilled through mountains. Tons of rock had to be chiseled out of hard ground and carried away. Few people wanted the jobs except immigrants, desperate for work. Many died in the transportation projects.

Building the Nation's Agriculture

Because some immigrants built the railroads, other immigrants could move west. Scandinavians and Germans were more successful at farming than the poorer Irish peasants. Some stayed in the cities, but many rode the trains to the rich farmlands of the West.

Thousands of them were drawn to the interior by the Homestead Act of 1862. Congress wanted people to settle and farm the West. So it passed laws that gave land away. The government gave people homesteads— 160 acres—at little or no cost. They had to live on the land and farm it for five years. To apply, a homesteader had to be a citizen or someone intending to become a citizen. Immigrants and nonimmigrants raced to Minnesota, Wisconsin, Kansas, Iowa, and Nebraska. Fifteen thousand families acquired land under the Homestead Act.[5] Records were not kept of how many of those were immigrants. Many of the names on the homestead applications, however, were German and Scandinavian.

German and Scandinavian immigrants settled in what would become the breadbasket of America. They farmed the wheat fields of the Midwest. They tilled the Mississippi and Missouri River valleys. They planted and harvested grain around the Great Lakes.

If the Midwest was the nation's breadbasket, California was its vegetable and fruit garden. And Chinese immigrants were partly responsible for California's agricultural wealth. When the transcontinental railroad was finished in 1869, thousands of Chinese were out of work. While some sought jobs in the cities, at least half went to the river valleys and deltas. They drained swamps and built irrigation canals so crops could be planted. They tended and picked the fruits and vegetables they had planted. Many became tenant farmers, working other people's land for a share of the crop. Some were able to save enough to buy their own farms.

Discrimination

Thus immigrants built the systems that moved and fed America. But not everyone seemed grateful. Some nonimmigrants, calling themselves nativists, were angry with the foreign-born, especially the Irish and Chinese. The nativists, children and grandchildren of immigrants themselves, disliked the more recent arrivals for several reasons.

For one, they were upset that the immigrants were willing to work for low pay. That kept the wages of everyone from rising. It also gave employers a way to control their workforces. Employers sometimes threatened to replace a problem employee with an immigrant who was willing to take the job. In the West, white workers blamed every economic problem on the

This drawing shows Chinese-American farmers working on a Louisiana sugar plantation in the 1870s.

Chinese. They were afraid the Chinese would take their jobs.

Some of the discrimination was due to racial and religious differences. Most nativists were Protestant and the Irish immigrants of the nineteenth century were Catholic. And some people were simply against anyone who was not white. Racial and religious prejudices were common in the 1800s.

These prejudices frequently boiled over into violence. Irish churches were burned down. Priests were cursed, stoned, and sometimes beaten. Chinese neighborhoods were raided often and innocent people were clubbed. Many were killed. In 1877, an anti-Chinese riot in San Francisco went on for three days. A year later, the white population of Truckee, California, chased all the Chinese people out of town. In 1880, an argument in a Chinese laundry in Denver turned into a riot. Every Chinese home and business in the city was completely destroyed.

These were the obvious incidents. But less obvious harassment went on daily. Irish and German workers were threatened at their jobs. One Chinese laundry-man described white men breaking into his business every week. They smashed windows, walked all over the laundry, and took money. "Every Saturday night," he said, "we never knew whether we would live to see the light of day."[6]

Local and state laws singled out the Chinese and made their lives difficult. A San Francisco sidewalk ordinance outlawed the way Chinese carried things. (They put a pole across their shoulders and balanced two baskets on the ends.) San Francisco also issued a queue ordinance. It forbade men from wearing their hair in braids (or queues), a Chinese custom. Chinese children were not allowed in public schools in California. Chinese people could not testify against white people in court.

Some nativists wanted laws like this for the entire country. They argued for more legal restrictions against immigrants. They wanted to bar foreign-born citizens from being elected to office. They suggested changing the residency requirement for naturalization from five to twenty-one years. In 1849, the nativists formed a political association to push for these changes. They called their group the American party.

In this political cartoon, the men on the left, representing members of the Know-Nothing party, are telling immigrants that they cannot be employed in Brooklyn, New York.

Others called the secretive association the Know-Nothing party. When members were asked questions about their party, they said they knew nothing.

Immigration Legislation

Despite nativists' feelings, immigration was not restricted during this period. In fact, the Fourteenth Amendment, adopted in 1868, helped some immigrants. It declared that "all persons born or naturalized in the United States" were citizens. No longer was citizenship restricted to free white persons. The amendment also meant that the children of immigrants were automatically citizens if they were born in the country. The children might even be Americans before their parents were eligible to apply for citizenship.

The Fourteenth Amendment had little immediate impact in the Asian community. Almost every Chinese person in America had been born overseas. Since most were men who expected to return to China, very few children were born to Chinese in the United States.

However, in the next few decades, more than 18 million people would take advantage of the many possibilities that America offered.

Defining America

By 1880, the United States was well established as a nation of immigrants. Irish policemen patrolled the streets of Boston and New York. Danish and Norwegian farms surrounded the lakes of Minnesota. Chinatowns dotted the cities of the West. German communities flourished in St. Louis, Cincinnati, and Milwaukee. Eighty percent of the population of New York, 84 percent of both Milwaukee and Detroit, and 87 percent of Chicago were immigrants and their children.[1]

Around 1890, however, the pattern of immigration changed. The countries that had sent so many immigrants in the past no longer had major "pushes." But the relative prosperity of northern and western Europe had not spread to southern Italy or Greece. Nor had it reached eastern Europe. There, overcrowding had led to massive poverty. Thousands of farmers were without land or work. They emigrated to escape extreme poverty. Some fled persecution.

One of the pulls that drew them to the United States was the great need for workers. In the mid- and late-nineteenth century, the Industrial Revolution swept across the United States. The economy had shifted from agriculture to manufacturing, or from growing crops to making things. The country needed workers for its factories.

The immigrants from southern and eastern Europe were largely unskilled in factory work. They had been farmers in their homelands. In the factories of America, they did not have to know how to read or write. They could learn the skills they would need. They did not even have to speak English. So, they came by the thousands.

The huge number of new arrivals overwhelmed city officials. Where would all these people live? Could they all find jobs? Before 1885, immigration had been restricted only for the Chinese. America was the home of the free, and people were free to come. Now,

These emigrants are traveling from Eastern Europe to America aboard the S.S. *Amsterdam*.

however, Congress began to limit who could come to the United States.

Laws passed in the 1880s barred certain types of people. Convicted criminals, the mentally ill, and those with contagious diseases, for example, could not enter the country. The government needed an agency to enforce these rules. So the Immigration Act of 1891 established a federal Bureau of Immigration.

Ellis Island

New York Harbor was known as "the Golden Door." It was the gate through which most European immigrants entered the country. On the busiest days, as many as ten thousand people arrived at the immigration station there.[2] An old army fort at Castle Garden, it could no longer handle the volume of people. On January 2, 1892, a new station for processing immigrants was opened on Ellis Island.

The processing actually began before the immigrants even reached the island. If a would-be immigrant was rejected, the shipping company that brought him or her to America had to take the immigrant back home. The company was charged a twenty-dollar fine for each "unwelcome visitor."[3] If the new arrival's entry was delayed for any reason, the shipping company had to pay for the immigrant's food while he or she waited. To avoid these costly possibilities, many shipping companies made sure their passengers seemed healthy enough to pass the American inspection.

Ellis Island served as a landing and processing station for immigrants from 1892 to 1954.

Being healthy when boarding, however, did not guarantee being healthy when arriving. Because they were poor, the new immigrants traveled in steerage. This meant they were in the cheapest accommodations, in the lower decks. They did not have cabins; they slept on bunks that lined the walls of the deck. Steerage decks, which were generally below sea level, got no light or air. Only when the hatches, the doors to the upper deck, were open could fresh air filter down. In any storm, the hatches had to remain closed. Sometimes the passengers spent days in the sunless steerage with the boat rolling violently. The decks were often packed with hundreds of bodies and reeked of seasickness.

Immigrants sometimes had to sleep in bunks in the steerage section below a ship's deck.

But when the journey ended, the Statue of Liberty invited the travelers ashore. Ellis Island was next to Lady Liberty. The weary yet hopeful immigrants filed off the ship and into the registry room. Most waited a long time for their turn at the front of one of the long lines. Inspectors had to pronounce them free from any noticeable illness.

The sick were ushered to the island's hospital. Some had to wait for relatives to come for them. They went to one of the many detention rooms. Those whose answers were not complete or were suspect were also detained. Some who had neither relatives nor money were helped by one of the many immigrant aid societies. Only about 2 percent were refused admittance.[4]

When the inspections and the detentions ended, the immigrants gathered their baggage, ate at one of the cafeterias, and exchanged their money for U.S. currency. Any who were going farther west or south could buy railroad tickets at an office on the island. Then, ferries carried them to New York City.

More than 12 million immigrants experienced America first at Ellis Island. But it was not the only processing center. Others were located in Boston, Philadelphia, and other Atlantic ports. An immigration station was built on the West Coast in 1905. It was located on Angel Island in China Cove, California.

Immigrants from Europe

Many of the new immigrants were Italian. They came from the rural south of Italy and the island of Sicily.

There, diseases, natural disasters, and worn-out land made life difficult. Overpopulation, unemployment, and heavy taxation made it unbearable for many. In the 1880s, more than three hundred thousand Italians immigrated to the United States. In the 1890s, the number more than doubled. And from 1900 to 1910, it was over 2 million.[5]

Immigrants also came from Italy's neighbor, Greece. They were driven by political turmoil, economic hardship, oppressive taxes, and a requirement to enlist in the military. Between 1900 and 1920, three hundred fifty thousand Greeks came to America looking for work.

These two southern European nations accounted for more than 4 million immigrants during the twentieth century. Another 5 million came from western Europe. More than half a million came from Asia and 1.5 million from the Americas. The largest group, nearly 6.5 million, was from eastern Europe. They were Czechs, Bohemians, Magyars, Slavs, Slovaks, Armenians, Serbs, Croats, Poles, Turks, Romanians, Bulgarians, Lithuanians, and Ukrainians.

One group in Russia and the countries it controlled emigrated because of prejudice. For the Jews of these nations, discrimination had grown into brutal persecution by 1890. Jews were not allowed to own land or hold certain jobs. They were often attacked by their neighbors or police. They were blamed for everything that went wrong. In the 1880s, the Russian government began killing Jews by the thousands and burning their homes. Those who survived fled in huge numbers. By 1920, more than a third of all the Jews of Russia had emigrated. About 3 million came to the United States.[6]

Immigrants from Asia

Eastern Europeans made up a large group, but they were not the only ones coming to America during this time. People were also arriving from Japan. For more than two centuries, Japan had been a closed society. Its rulers had intentionally isolated their country from all Western influence. But in 1853, Commodore Matthew Perry took U.S. Navy gunships into Tokyo Bay. He gave ordinary Japanese citizens a glimpse of life outside Japan. Many liked what they saw.

In the next few decades, new rulers scrambled to modernize Japan. They were afraid the stronger Western powers would carve their islands up into colonies as they had in China. Their strategy was to industrialize Japan to make it strong economically.

This rapid modernization turned Japanese society upside down. The government had to charge heavy taxes to pay for the new factories and armies. The people could not pay the taxes. Farmers had to give up their lands. They fled to the cities to find jobs. The sudden increase in workers pushed wages to very low levels. The abandoned farmlands could not produce enough food and thousands went hungry. In their misery, the Japanese listened eagerly to stories of jobs and riches in the United States.

However, The Japanese government maintained strict control of its emigration. Officials allowed only healthy people of good character to leave. They wanted their representatives in foreign lands to "maintain Japan's national honor."[7] Beginning in the 1880s, large numbers were permitted to leave. About half went to the sugar plantations of Hawaii. (Hawaii did not become an American territory until 1898. It became a state in 1959). Almost the same number went to the American West Coast.

Immigrants from North America

The Atlantic and Pacific coasts were not the only points of entry into the United States. During the century of immigration, people came south from Canada and north from Mexico.

The immigrants from Canada were mostly from the French-speaking province of Quebec. They were "pushed" south by a growing population and poor soil. Like so many others, they came in search of economic opportunity. They found that opportunity in the textile mills and other factories of New England. Because there was no processing center to receive them, the number of French-Canadian immigrants is unknown. Census figures show that about four hundred thousand settled in the United States between the years of 1890 and 1920.[8]

The number of immigrants from Mexico is just as difficult to determine. Mexicans and Mexican

Americans moved back and forth across the border freely. Large-scale immigration did not begin until 1911. In that year, long-standing discontent with Mexico's president bubbled up into a revolution. For the next twenty years, great unrest rocked the country. Assassinations, fighting, and bloodshed were common.

Two factors pulled Mexicans to the United States. One was its location. Hindered only by the Rio Grande, people from Mexico could come north easily. The greatest draw, however, was the promise of higher wages. In the 1920s, an unskilled worker could earn $18 a month in Mexico versus $105 a month in the United States.[9] Before 1900, the highest number of Mexicans entering the United States in any decade was sixty-six hundred. In the two decades between 1910 and 1930, the figure was more than one hundred times that number.[10]

But that was only the official figure. Many Mexicans slipped across the border without going through any legal process. Some swam the Rio Grande. Some snuck across at night. Others were brought by *coyotes*, men who smuggled people across the border for a fee.

Some of these immigrants did not intend to stay. They simply wanted to make enough money to feed their families. They planned to return to Mexico when conditions there got better. At least a million of the early Mexican immigrants did go back across the border.[11]

Living and Working in America

Some of the immigrants, such as those from Mexico, lived in rural areas. The Czechs, the Russian Mennonites, and some others went to the farms of the Midwest. However, the majority of the immigrants in the East lived in cities. Most did not have money for decent housing. So several families crammed together in tenements. A tenement is a home built for one family that has been divided up and rented out to many people. Poor immigrants lived in the rooms, cellars, attics, or sheds of tenements. The poorest lived in alleys. The tiny, cramped living quarters frequently lacked running water, proper sewage, and any privacy. They bred disease.

The various national groups usually clustered together in the same block or the same building. So several cities had, for example, a "Little Italy," a "Bohemian Village," a "Turkish Town," and other ethnic ghettos. The Italians, fiercely loyal to their villages, banded together according to the province in Italy from which they came.

Living in close-knit ethnic communities made obtaining jobs easier. When one person found a willing employer, his neighbors applied at the same place. Slavs tended to work in the coal mines, Russian Jews in garment factories, Italians in construction and public works. If they could not find jobs, they made their own. Some immigrants became shoemakers, barbers, street vendors, or peddlers. Many of the women and children toiled in sweatshops. Sweatshops were factories with poor working conditions, long hours, and low wages.

Conditions in the urban slums were bleak. But the ghettos offered some comfort to people who were confused and frightened in a foreign world. They were with neighbors who spoke their language and shared their values and interests. Immigrants could read newspapers and enjoy performances in their native tongue. They could buy food prepared as it was in their homeland. Familiar social, cultural, and religious organizations helped ease the transition to their new lives.

In the West, immigrants also clustered together. The Mexican Americans who worked in cities lived in neighborhoods called *barrios*. The Southwest was dotted with large, Spanish-speaking barrios. El Paso, San Diego, Los Angeles—all hosted Mexican immigrant communities.

Likewise, the Chinese formed compact, colorful neighborhoods. They became known as Chinatowns. Self-help groups sprang up in these neighborhoods. They were started by family groups or business owners. These groups helped people find jobs and housing. They settled disagreements and helped with legal problems. They organized the festivals and celebrations that helped the people retain their culture.

Secret societies also arose in the Chinatowns. Called *tongs*, these groups were sometimes involved in criminal activity. They controlled the opium trade, gambling, and prostitution that went on in the shadows. Sometimes violence flared between rival tongs.

For the most part, however, the close-knit communities were islands of comfort to the Chinese in the cities of America.

Japanese immigrants needed the same kind of comfort. For those in the sugarcane fields of Hawaii, work was long and difficult. Housing was poor, and bosses could be harsh. The plantation owners hired Japanese, Chinese, Korean, and Filipino laborers and kept the groups separate. Often, they pitted the groups against one another.

Like the Chinese in California, the Japanese in Hawaii formed their own communities. They published Japanese newspapers and built Japanese schools, stores, and churches. They even put together Japanese baseball teams. And they prospered. Although treated unfairly by their white employers,

This is the gateway to Chinatown in San Francisco, California, as it looks today.

they did not face terrible discrimination on the streets. Most of the population of the islands was Asian. By 1923, Japanese made up more than half of that population.

On the mainland, however, in California, the Japanese were treated much like the Chinese. They found jobs as farm laborers and in mines, canneries, and railroads. Also like the Chinese, they proved to be good workers, clean, and well behaved. They were thrifty. Many saved their wages and bought farms. Others opened small businesses that grew.

Targets of Blame

The work the immigrants found often put them in direct contact, and often direct conflict, with nonimmigrants. When anything went wrong, people were quick to blame immigrants. And much went wrong in the 1890s and early 1900s.

This was a period of labor unrest. Workers protested intolerable conditions. Union strikes and employer lockouts were common. Employers often brought in low-paid immigrants to break the strikes. The immigrants, merely trying to make a living, were blamed for the labor problems.

The 1890s and 1900s were times of economic crisis. Business failures caused the stock market to collapse. This triggered an economic panic in 1893. The panic turned into a severe nationwide depression. A million workers lost their jobs.[12] People blamed immigrants.

The depression occurred during a time of political

fraud. Politics in some cities were controlled by political machines. The most famous machine was the Irish-run Tammany Hall in New York City. A political machine is a group of people who get enough supporters to take control of the day-to-day operation of a city. The "bosses" who run the group give jobs and other favors to their supporters. The supporters vote for whoever or whatever the bosses say. The political

Famous Immigrant
Knute Rockne, Football Coach
(1888–1931)

Knute Rockne was only five when his family moved from Norway to Chicago. As a child, he added to the family income by washing windows, picking beets and corn, and making deliveries for a store. In school, Knute excelled in sports. He was a runner. He held his school's pole-vaulting record. But his favorite sport was football.

Seven years after quitting high school, Rockne enrolled at Notre Dame College. At only five feet eight inches and 160 pounds, he was not chosen right away for the school's football team. But eventually he played. Later, he coached the team.

When Rockne started coaching, football was not a particularly popular sport. But he perfected two little-used strategies: the shift and the forward pass. These revolutionized the game. In his thirteen years as head coach of the "Fighting Irish" of Notre Dame, the team had an amazing record of 105 wins, 12 losses, and 5 ties. It was undefeated in five seasons. "The Rock" became an American hero.

Knute Rockne died in a plane crash at age forty-three.

machines were riddled with bribery, kickbacks, and theft. They made life hard for honest citizens. Because the bosses recruited and rewarded immigrants for their votes, immigrants were blamed for political corruption.

They were also blamed for all the misery of life in crowded cities. Urban decay, crime, fires, accidents— all were seen as the fault of immigrants. They were even blamed for the poor conditions in the factories where they worked.

Immigrants were blamed for a wave of fear and violence that swept the country from 1919 to 1921. After the Russian Revolution, Americans worried that Communists, known as Reds, would try to take over the United States. A small group of radicals and anarchists seemed to support that idea. Some immigrants belonged to this small group. In 1919, a string of bombings set off a "Red Scare." People believed that radicals wanted to start a Communist revolution in the United States. They connected any crime, any problem with the radicals. And they assumed that all immigrants were radicals. All over the country, riots, raids, and mob violence fanned the hysteria.

The most well known example of anti-immigrant feeling occurred in 1920. Two men were murdered and fifteen thousand dollars was stolen from a factory in Massachusetts. Two Italian immigrants, Nicola Sacco and Bartolomeo Vanzetti, were arrested. They denied committing the crime. The judge was openly prejudiced against the two men. Many jurors were obviously

A Russian family is ready to start a new life in New York.

biased. The evidence against the men was flimsy. Still, Sacco and Vanzetti were pronounced guilty and sentenced to death. Appeals dragged on for seven years. Even though another man confessed in 1925, Sacco and Vanzetti were executed in 1927.

Becoming American

Despite the anti-immigrant mood, the new arrivals succeeded in making America their home. They got jobs that took them out of their ethnic communities and into the American world. They learned the English language. They became citizens and voted. Their children went to public schools. They became interested in sports, entertainment, and politics. They shared their art, their talents, and their native cooking with others.

They adopted some of the customs of their neighbors. And their neighbors copied some of their ways. In one sense, they assimilated, or became part of American society. In another sense, they helped shape America.

Some moved into the mainstream of American life more quickly than others. In school, the children of immigrants picked up the English language and American customs fairly rapidly. They wanted to be

Famous Immigrant
Father Edward Flanagan, Priest
(1886–1948)

Edward Flanagan came from Ireland in 1904. He was eighteen years old. He became a priest in 1912. Seven years later, he became a U.S. citizen.

Father Flanagan was assigned to a church in Omaha, Nebraska. There, he was troubled by the sight of hundreds of unemployed men, homeless in the bitter Nebraska winters. He set up the Workingmen's Hotel as a shelter for them. Even more troubling, he found many boys who were also homeless. He turned a large abandoned house into a home for them.

When the boys' house was full, Father Flanagan built a bigger shelter ten miles from Omaha. The project grew into an entire town. It took in boys from every nationality, every religion. The boys built the town and helped govern it. In 1936, Boys' Town became an official Nebraska city.

Boys' Town is a thriving city today. It has its own hospitals, schools, workshops, and post office. A number of Boys' Towns have been built in other countries. The 1938 movie *Boys' Town* starring Spencer Tracy and Mickey Rooney tells Father Flanagan's story.

like their classmates. Thus many children became Americanized more quickly than their parents. This created tension in many homes. Parents were troubled that their sons and daughters could so easily shed the old traditions. Often the children could function better in the larger society than the adults. This sometimes forced them to reverse their roles in the family. The children became translators and go-betweens for their parents.

Some parents, although they very much wanted to be American, also wanted to keep the customs and values of their home countries. They did not actually want to assimilate; they wanted to be accepted. Many would never feel fully accepted. But the hope of some was that their children would one day be known simply as American.

Many did. Within one or two generations, prejudices faded. Some once-poor immigrants were able to climb the ladder of social and economic success. As they did, they gave to their adopted country much more than the colorful customs and traditions of their native lands. This group helped define America as more than a nation of immigrants. They made it a land of many cultures and many peoples.

America Restricts Immigration

The many cultures and many peoples that made America sometimes also made for conflict. That conflict often showed up as discrimination. Sometimes it turned into riots. In the late 1800s, it resulted in anti-immigrant feelings among some. The feelings were so strong that many called for the government to stop or at least restrict immigration.

Until 1875, the federal government did not regulate immigration. For a long time, no one put limits on who could come into the country. People came and went freely. After the Civil War ended in 1865, a few people wanted some controls on immigration. At that time, each state decided who could enter the country by crossing one of its borders. Some states made laws that set limits on who could be admitted. But people could enter the country in one state and then travel to another. So in 1875, the Supreme Court put the federal government in charge of immigration.

After the Civil War, America's economy went into a

Statue of Liberty

Originally titled "Liberty Enlightening the World," the statue was a gift from France. It was meant to mark the United States' hundredth birthday in 1876, but it was not finished until

1886. The people of France spent $400,000 to build the 152-foot-tall statue. Americans raised $270,000 to pay for the 86-foot pedestal, or base, on which it stands. The lady, who represents liberty, holds a book engraved with the date "July 4, 1776." Broken chains lie at her feet. They stand for tyrants whose power is broken when people become free.

When the gift was given, no one thought about immigrants. France wanted it to remind French and Americans of their friendship. France and America were two of the very few countries that were democratic at that time. Many nations were still ruled by kings or emperors. The statue, placed in New York Harbor, was supposed to "enlighten" people in other countries. It was meant to encourage them to rise up against unjust rulers as French and Americans had done.

American poet Emma Lazarus changed the meaning of the statue. In 1883, she wrote a poem called "The New Colossus." It was part of the effort to raise money for the statue's pedestal. Of the poem's fourteen lines, the last five have become famous:

> Give me your tired, your poor,
> Your huddled masses yearning to breathe free,
> The wretched refuse of your teeming shore
> Send these, the homeless, tempest-tost to me,
> I lift my lamp beside the golden door.

The statue was no longer about encouraging people to make their countries free. Instead, it was an invitation to enjoy the freedom of the United States. It became the hope of immigrants everywhere.

depression. Some businesses failed and jobs were lost. Panicked workers feared that immigrants would take their jobs. This fear, combined with racial prejudice, led to immigration restrictions.

Chinese Exclusion

The first legal restrictions on immigration fell on the Chinese. In 1882, Congress passed the Chinese Exclusion Act. This law said that no Chinese would be allowed to enter the United States for ten years. In 1892, Congress renewed the ban for another ten years. In 1902, Congress declared the ban permanent.

Some Chinese were able to get around the restriction. The law permitted Chinese merchants, students, and diplomats to enter the country. For a time, these excepted immigrants were allowed to bring their wives and families. A number of young Chinese passed themselves off as family members. They bought papers that identified them, inaccurately, as children of people eligible to be in the country. They were known as "paper sons" and "paper daughters."

To enforce the Chinese Exclusion Act, the federal government established an immigration station on the California coast. It was located on Angel Island in a harbor called China Cove. Its purpose was to process immigrants, but it was basically a detention center, or a temporary jail. Officials quizzed the paper children. These clever immigrants had memorized details of "their families'" lives. They knew their history, ancestors, and relatives. Checking their stories sometimes

In this room at the Angel Island station, male immigrants slept while they were waiting to have their paperwork processed.

took weeks or months. A few had to live in the detention barracks for almost two years. During the time Angel Island was open, between 1910 and 1940, one hundred seventy-five thousand Chinese managed to get into the United States.[1]

Although none of the paper sons or daughters could become Americans, their children could. Under U.S. law, any child born in the United States is automatically a U.S. citizen. So despite the blatant attempts to exclude the Chinese, the number of Chinese in America grew.

Restrictions on Japanese

Like the Chinese, the Japanese in the United States could not become citizens. When hard economic times fell, white Americans wanted them to leave. Labor union leaders barred them from membership in their unions. California passed the Alien Land Law, which said that no noncitizen could own land. The Japanese had to give up land they had bought years earlier.

The government of Japan did not want to suffer the same humiliation China had. So its leaders negotiated a "gentleman's agreement," which was approved in

Famous Immigrant
I. M. Pei, Architect
(1917–)

Born in Canton, China, Ieoh Ming Pei also lived in Shanghai and Hong Kong. Ieoh came to the United States in 1934, at age seventeen, to study architecture. He planned to return to China, but in 1939, China was at war with Japan. So I. M. Pei stayed in the United States.

Pei is one of the most successful architects in the United States. He designs large buildings with lots of concrete and glass. He became well known when he designed the John F. Kennedy Library in Boston. Of the nearly fifty projects he has designed, more than half have won prestigious awards.

Pei has used his fame and his award money to benefit his native country. He has supported efforts to bring greater democracy to China. And he established a scholarship fund for Chinese who want to study architecture in the United States and return to China to practice.

Of his many awards, he cherishes the Medal of Liberty presented by President Ronald Reagan. He says it shows that he, an immigrant, has been accepted by the people of his adopted country.

1908. Japan agreed to stop general emigration to America. In return, the United States agreed to allow entry to wives, children, and other relatives of Japanese already in the country. Still, Japanese could not become citizens.

However, their children could. Unlike the Chinese, the Japanese had been able to come to the United States with their families. So children were born to many Japanese in America. Those in the second generation, called Nisei, were American citizens. As in Hawaii, the Japanese on the mainland adjusted to their alien status. But their gradual progress toward acceptance was abruptly halted by World War II.

Within hours of Japan's attack on the U.S. fleet in Pearl Harbor, Japanese were being arrested as security

This Japanese-American family is being evacuated from San Francisco to an internment camp.

risks. A hysterical public was afraid that any Japanese could be a spy or an enemy agent. So they were forced to move to internment camps hundreds of miles from their homes. During the course of the war, one hundred twenty-five thousand Japanese from the West Coast were relocated to the inland prisons.[2]

Despite this mistreatment, many Nisei distinguished themselves while their parents remained interned. More than three hundred thousand Japanese Americans enlisted in the military during the war. One all-Japanese unit received over eighteen thousand individual medals.[3] These were some of the people the nativists would have kept out of the country.

General Restrictions

For many nativists, restricting Asian immigrants was not enough. They wanted limits on all foreign-born people. A group calling itself the Immigration Restriction League brought the matter before Congress. The issue was hotly debated for twenty-two years. On one side were nativists claiming that too many immigrants were lazy, inferior, and dangerous. On the other side were politicians who were willing to give everyone a chance at the American dream.

The topic came up again in 1917. That was during the height of World War I. At that time, antiforeign sentiment was especially strong. Many Americans were isolationists. They wanted America to stay out of anything foreign. They also wanted anything foreign to stay out of America. That included immigrants. This

Sometimes immigrants were not allowed to enter the country. Here, a man is detained at Ellis Island in 1911.

time, the argument in Congress for restriction of immigrants won.

The Immigration Act of 1917 was the first serious attempt to limit who could be admitted to the United States. Previous laws banned people with mental disorders, people with contagious diseases, and others who were obvious threats to public safety. Prior laws barred those who might become burdens to society. But the 1917 decree affected ordinary, law-abiding people. It required that they prove they could read and write before being allowed to enter the country. If a family was attempting to immigrate, only the head of the household had to pass the literacy test. The test was not an English test; instead, it could be given in any language.

The 1917 law probably did not keep many would-be immigrants out. But it was a victory for people who wanted restriction. And they kept fighting for greater limits. Their next success came in 1921. Congress passed a new measure. It was only temporary, but it was a radical departure from all previous policies.

The Emergency Quota Act of 1921 set an immigration quota for each foreign country. This is how the quota was figured. The year 1910 was used as a baseline. Take Germany, for example. The number of people in the United States in 1910 who had been born in Germany was calculated. The number of new immigrants admitted each year from Germany could not be more than 3 percent of that number. The law did not apply to every country. It completely ignored the Western Hemisphere. That meant it did not apply to Canada or Mexico. It did not mention Asian countries because Asian immigration was already restricted. It applied mostly to Europe.

National Origins Act

Three years later, a much stricter law was passed. The National Origins Act of 1924 established permanent immigration quotas. It dropped the percentage from 3 to 2 percent. And it moved the baseline back to 1890. Before 1890, very few southern and eastern Europeans were in the United States. In effect, the law stopped immigration from those regions. It also declared the gentleman's agreement with Japan no longer valid. Thus it also stopped immigration from Japan.

The 1924 legislation required every immigrant to have a visa. A visa is a form that shows the immigrant's legal status. Visas are issued in a U.S. office in a foreign country. A person coming to the United States from a nation that had a quota would have a "quota visa." Someone from a country without a quota would have a "non-quota visa." Visas were also labeled "immigrant" or "nonimmigrant," depending on whether the holder was applying to live in America or just visiting. Eventually, more categories would be added, such as "student visas" and "work visas."

The National Origins Act of 1924 marked the end of the century of immigration. The day of nearly unlimited access to America was over. The act, however, did not end immigration. It merely slowed it. And it slowed it only temporarily.

Immigration Slows

The laws of the 1920s did less to slow immigration than the Great Depression of the 1930s. During the Depression, which was worldwide, many people could not find jobs. America was no exception. It had no pull for foreigners. In fact, between 1932 and 1935, more people left the United States than came in. Many returned to their native lands.[1]

Immigration from Mexico

Some of the emigrants did not leave voluntarily. They were the ones who had come from Mexico. The Great Depression had left many Americans hungry and out of work. Some resented Mexican immigrants having food and jobs. So the government rounded up Mexicans who were not U.S. citizens. They put them on trains and sent them back to Mexico. Some immigrants who had become U.S. citizens were also placed on the deportation trains.[2]

The Mexican Americans who remained in the United States had a hard time during the Depression. Many employers had to lay off workers. Farm laborers traveled from field to field, looking for work. The federal government set up migrant camps in areas where Mexican Americans tended to go. In the camps, the farmworkers had a safe place to stay and food to eat.

The Great Depression ended with America's entry into World War II in December 1941. The conflict pulled young men from the fields and factories to fight overseas. Employers, especially farmers, looked for workers to fill their jobs. To meet that need, the governments of the United States and Mexico developed a *bracero* program. A *bracero* is a guest worker with a contract to work in the United States for a period of time. Most worked in the fields during the harvesting season. The braceros were usually paid very little. Their living and working conditions were often harsh.

Mexican workers were hired by the Farm Service Administration in the 1940s to harvest sugar beets.

Still, for most, this was better than what Mexico offered at the time.

Not all the immigrants worked in the fields. Factory jobs were open now, and many from Mexico made their way into the cities of the West and Midwest. As with other immigrants living in crowded ghettos, Mexican Americans faced prejudice and discrimination in the cities. Sometimes the prejudice led to violence.

Such was the case in Los Angeles in 1943. In that city, some second-generation Mexican-American youths had formed street gangs. They were easily identified by their unusual attire: the zoot suit. They wore baggy pants tied at the ankles. Their jackets were loose, hanging to the knees, and had wide, padded shoulders. They had broad-brimmed hats and long watch chains. A group of sailors claimed the zoot suitors had attacked them. They went on a rampage in the barrios of Los Angeles. They beat anyone who looked Mexican. For five days the carnage raged and the police did little. It ended with sailors being banned from the city and the wearing of zoot suits prohibited.

The ending of the zoot suit riot did not stop the tension between immigrants and nonimmigrants. When World War II ended and there was no longer a labor shortage in the United States, many people wanted to send the workers back to Mexico. Food growers, however, wanted them to stay. The Mexican laborers were willing to work longer hours for less pay than others. The government compromised. It extended the bracero program until 1964 and at the same time deported 4 million Mexican immigrants.[3]

Refugees from War

While Mexicans crossed the border relatively easily, some Europeans wanted desperately to reach America's shores. In the 1930s, many Germans, especially German Jews, were seeking safety. Adolf Hitler had come to power in Germany in 1933. His Nazi government was persecuting many who disagreed with him. The Nazis put Jews and others into concentration camps. Many feared for their lives. Thousands of Germans looked to the United States, as well as other countries, for help.

But the United States did not want to help. As in World War I, many political leaders were isolationists. They did not want to get involved in another country's problems. And they certainly did not want to bring what they considered another country's problems to the United States. Besides, the Jewish people asking for help were not allowed to take their money out of Germany. So they would be financial burdens in America. Such persons could be excluded from entry into the United States.

The people fleeing Germany were seeking refuge, or safety. American immigration law had no way to deal with refugees. And no one seemed willing to make any exception for the German Jews. Even when the *Saint Louis,* a ship filled with almost a thousand refugees, tried to land in Florida, it was turned away.

After World War II, many Jewish people had no homes to which to return. This six-year-old orphan waits for his name to be called at the Buchenwald camp in Germany after the war. The boy is about to leave for Switzerland.

Famous Immigrant
Albert Einstein, Physicist
(1879–1955)

Born in Germany, Albert Einstein began learning to play the violin at age six. He taught himself geometry at age twelve. He studied physics on his own. He is best known for his theory of relativity. He received many awards for his research. In 1922, he won the Nobel Prize in physics.

Einstein was interested in two political causes. He was a pacifist, which means he was against warfare. And he was a Jew who wanted Jews to have their own country. These were dangerous stands to take in Germany in the 1930s.

Because he was famous, Einstein traveled to different countries to speak. He came to the United States in December 1932 to work at Princeton University for a few months. In January, Hitler came to power in Germany. Einstein did not go back. He became a U.S. citizen in 1940. He continued to work for a Jewish nation in Israel and for world peace.

Albert Einstein received his certificate of American citizenship from Judge Phillip Forman on October 1, 1940.

Under the 1924 National Origins Act, 211,895 Germans could immigrate from 1933 to 1940.[4] This was far less than the hundreds of thousands attempting to come. Still, the quotas for those years were not filled. In all the 1930s, only 114,000 Germans were admitted to the United States.[5] They were not the common people like those on the *Saint Louis*. Many were people of influence. They were scholars, scientists, and artists. Others, like the Burgers, were sponsored by relatives in the United States or by private organizations.

Refugees were not recognized in immigration law until World War II was over. After the war, much of Europe was devastated. Thousands of people were without homes or jobs. They lived in displaced persons camps. Some sought to rebuild their lives in other countries, including the United States. The entire world was moved by their plight. America decided to open its doors a little wider to receive them. Congress passed the Displaced Persons Act in 1948 and the Refugee Relief Act in 1953. These laws made exceptions to the National Origins Act quotas. They allowed some war refugees to enter even if the quotas from their countries were full.

Changes for Asians

World War II also affected how the United States thought of Asians. China was America's ally in the conflict. Thirteen thousand Chinese fought in the war in American uniforms. Less than half were American citizens.[6] Many had volunteered for service because Japan, one of America's enemies in the war, had invaded China. U.S. officials were embarrassed to have a law that forbade its allies access to their country. The Chinese Exclusion Act, in effect for sixty-one years, was finally repealed in 1943.

The repeal of the Chinese Exclusion law did not affect immigration significantly. It allowed only 105 Chinese immigrants to enter the country each year.[7] Perhaps more importantly, it permitted Chinese to apply for citizenship. The sons and daughters of the men who had opened the West, who had planted and harvested its fruits and vegetables, could finally call themselves Americans.

Two years after the Chinese were granted the right to become citizens, that same privilege was opened to Filipinos. Filipinos had been in a unique category since 1898. In that year, the Philippines had become an American territory. Its people were American "nationals." They could travel freely throughout the United States. But they could not be U.S. citizens because they were not white. Like the Chinese, many Filipinos fought alongside the United States in World War II. In 1946, the Philippines became independent. Filipinos then became eligible for U.S. citizenship.

These changes in immigration policy did not seriously raise the numbers of immigrants. The number had dropped sharply after the quotas of the National Origins Act went into effect. Immigration in the 1930s was only 12 percent of what it was in the 1920s. The new laws of the 1940s brought it up to 25 percent of the 1920s figures. The older legislation had slowed the movement of people into the country considerably. But in the years to follow, events in a number of countries would turn many more people toward America. And changes in U.S. law would allow them in. Immigration would increase so sharply that the 1990s would see more people enter the country than in any previous decade.[8]

7

Changing Patterns of Immigration

For almost three hundred fifty years after the first settlements in America, the bulk of immigration to the new country came from Europe. In the second half of the twentieth century, the pattern of immigration changed. Europeans still came, but the numbers from Asia jumped dramatically. Since the 1960s, more people have entered the United States from North and South American countries than from any other part of the globe. The pushes and the pulls of this changing pattern are as many and as varied as the number of countries involved.

The Immigration Act of 1965 allowed the patterns to change. This law did away with the quota system based on national origin. In its place were limits on the numbers of immigrants from the Eastern and Western hemispheres. The law gave preferences to relatives of U.S. citizens and relatives of noncitizens who were permanent residents of the United States. It also gave preference to refugees.

Asians

The Immigration Act was a great boon for Asians. Gone were the caps of one to two hundred immigrants per country. Gone was the exclusion of any national group. The thousands of Chinese and Japanese already in the country could send for other members of their families. More Chinese than Japanese took advantage of the new opportunities. By 1965, Japan was prospering economically. Most Japanese were happy to remain in Japan.

To the south of Japan, in the Philippines, a number of people were not happy. Political and economic uncertainty caused many Filipinos to emigrate. Between 1965 and 1984, six hundred thirty thousand came to the United States.[1] Most were professionals, many in the medical fields. Many U.S. hospitals invited Filipino nurses to work in America. In a number of years, people from the Philippines made up the largest immigrant group.

A smaller number of Asians have come from Korea. The first group of any size consisted of war brides. These were Korean women married to American servicemen. They came after the Korean conflict of 1950–1953. Like the Chinese, Japanese, and Filipino immigrants, most of the Koreans settled in the western United States. Los Angeles has a thriving Koreatown.

One Asian group that is scattered throughout the country comes from India. In the early 1900s, poor Asians from the Punjab region of India settled on farms in California. Wealthier Indian merchants lived on both the East and West coasts. After 1965, educated Indian professionals immigrated. Like so many others, they were looking for economic betterment. Many started their own businesses.

Southeast Asians

A decade after the 1965 Immigration Act sparked a boom in Asian immigration, people began arriving from Southeast Asia. They were refugees from the Vietnam War. When U.S. soldiers left Vietnam in 1975, Communists from North Vietnam took over South Vietnam. Many Vietnamese, Cambodians, and Laotians had fought against the Communists. They were afraid the Communists would kill them for their part in the war. The Hmong, a mountain tribe of Laos, had fought alongside the American soldiers. They, too, feared for their lives. In the last days of the war, Americans airlifted as many of its allies out of the region as it could. Thousands more fled to refugee camps in Thailand. They waited there for the chance to move to the West.

Within four years after the war ended, four hundred thousand Southeast Asian immigrants were in the United States. By 2000, more than 1.6 million were U.S. citizens.[2] The last large group of war refugees came in the summer of 2004. At that time, more than fifteen thousand Hmong who had been living in Thailand were finally admitted to the United States.[3]

Mexicans

Rising numbers of people from Asia were one of the new immigration patterns of the twentieth century. Another was an increase from the Western Hemisphere.

For Mexicans, the pull to America was the promise of employment. Economic conditions in the United States were generally far better than in Mexico. Mexicans continued to come north where they could earn more. Millions came in the 1980s and 1990s, more than from all European countries combined. Millions more came illegally, driven by poverty, drawn by the hope of making money. Many believe that the number of illegal Mexican immigrants is higher than the number of those in the country legally.[4]

The illegal immigrants are sometimes called undocumented aliens. They do not have the documents that show they have a legal right to be in the country. The documents are important because employers need them to put people on their payrolls. Some get around this problem by using forged papers. Others use the identifications of friends or relatives who were once in the United States legally but returned to Mexico. Many others pay their Mexican employees cash, eliminating the need for payrolls or documents.

The presence of so many illegal immigrants has posed a thorny problem. On the one hand, they have obviously broken the law. They are living in the country without permission and use American services such as schools, medical care, and public assistance. On the other hand, they probably contribute enough to the economy to more than pay for those services.[5] Another concern is that any child born in the United States is automatically a U.S. citizen. This means that many illegal aliens have "legal" children. Where should these families live? These questions are still unanswered.

Immigrant Olympic Team

Five of the seven members of the U.S. 2004 Olympic table tennis team were immigrants. Two were from Vietnam, two from the former Yugoslavia, and one from China. One of the nonimmigrant team members was the daughter of Cambodian immigrants.

Khoa Nguyen was nine years old when Communist North Vietnam overran South Vietnam. He escaped with all his family except two sisters. It would be several years before he would see them. Khoa's father taught him how to play table tennis because he thought it would help him forget all the pain he had experienced.

The other Vietnamese team member, Tawny Banh, spent a year in a refugee camp in Malaysia before immigrating to the United States. She became a citizen at age eighteen.

The two table tennis players from Yugoslavia are Ilija Lupulesku and Jasna Reed. Both played in previous Olympics for their native country. Jasna won a bronze medal and gave it to her grandmother. The grandmother lost the medal when soldiers raided her town. Jasna wants to win another medal for her grandmother.

Gao Jun Chang was born in China. She won a silver medal for China in the 1992 Olympics. After becoming a U.S. citizen in 1997, she dreamed of winning again. Getting another medal was not important to her. What she wanted was to win for her new country.

Puerto Ricans

While some people from Mexico were coming secretly into the United States, another group was entering the country openly. They were from the American territory of Puerto Rico, about one thousand miles southeast of Florida. Puerto Ricans have been American citizens since the United States acquired the island in 1917. Puerto Rico is not a state, but a commonwealth. Puerto Ricans are American citizens and are free to come and go anywhere in the country. But for nearly thirty years, very few left the island.

After World War II, however, they began to come to the mainland at the rate of twenty-five thousand a year.[6] Their island is very crowded. Yet because of its isolation, many Puerto Ricans were poor. Wages were higher in New York. At that time, airlines were competing for customers. They offered a flight from Puerto Rico to New York for as little as thirty-five dollars.

The Puerto Rican flag is red, white, and blue, just like the American flag. Puerto Ricans are American citizens and do not need passports to travel to the American mainland.

A person could earn that much in a week in New York City's garment factories, hotels, or hospitals.[7] Even though Florida was closer, the cheap airline fare brought Puerto Ricans to New York.

They came, not as immigrants, but as migrants. Their experience, however, was much the same as that of the Eastern European immigrant. The majority put down roots where they landed: in New York City. Northeast Manhattan became known as Spanish

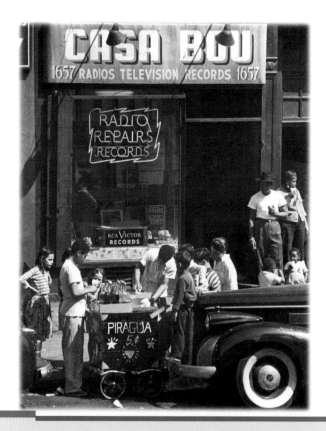

Latino children line up for a special type of ice dessert called *piragua* in the Spanish Harlem section of New York City in 1950.

Harlem. The Puerto Ricans lived in tenement-like housing in inner-city barrios. They began on the bottom of the employment ladder. They had to learn English. They encountered prejudice and discrimination.

But again, like many of the Eastern European immigrants, some of the second-generation Puerto Ricans rose above their circumstances. They built community centers, schools, churches, and businesses. They entered politics and gained fame in sports, literature, and entertainment. Today almost as many Puerto Ricans live on the mainland as in Puerto Rico.[8]

Cubans

Closer to the United States than Puerto Rico is the island nation of Cuba. In 1959, Fidel Castro took over Cuba and installed a Communist government. The island, once thought of as an Atlantic paradise, was filled with soldiers, forced-labor camps, and firing squads. Thousands fled, most to the United States. The majority settled in Miami, Florida.

Cuban immigration started and stopped as Cuban-American relations warmed or cooled. People who had lost their positions in Castro's revolution were among the first to immigrate. They feared for their lives. Many were from the wealthy and middle classes. They flew to the United States before commercial flights were halted in 1962. They hoped their stay would be temporary. They waited for their chance to overthrow Castro and restore their country.

But that chance did not come. Castro, with the

backing of the powerful Soviet Union, retained firm control. And conditions in Cuba worsened. By 1980, the island's economy was ruined. Jobs, housing, and food were in short supply. In a sudden surprise move, Castro opened the tiny fishing port of Mariel to Cubans wishing to leave. The Cuban-American community in Florida was anxious to bring friends and relatives out of Cuba. Cubans in Miami rushed every boat they could find to Mariel. Commercial boats, pleasure craft, fishing vessels—anything that could float was pressed into service. The rescuers had no idea how long Castro would keep the door open.

The boat lift was allowed to go on for about two months. The boats were crammed with desperate people. Many of the vessels were not seaworthy. Some did not have enough life jackets. The U.S. Navy and Coast Guard helped ships that ran out of gas. They escorted vessels through storms. They picked up people whose boats could not make the ninety-mile trip. When it was over, one hundred twenty-five thousand new Cuban immigrants had landed in Key West, Florida.[9]

When Castro closed the harbor, people still came. They escaped on homemade boats, thin wooden rafts, and inner tubes. They risked drowning, exposure to scorching sun and biting wind, and sharks. Some died in the attempt. The United States did not want to encourage such dangerous actions. So at the end of the 1990s, the American government announced that no boats from Cuba would be allowed to reach shore.

Still, people came. One little raft made international

These Cuban immigrants tried to reach the United States by attaching empty barrels to a truck body so that it would float.

news in 1999. Everyone on the boat was washed overboard and drowned except one six-year-old boy. Elián Gonzales was rescued and taken to his cousin in Miami. That would have been the end of the story except that Elián's father was still in Cuba. He had not given the boy's mother permission to take him to America, and he wanted him back. For seven months the little immigrant was the center of a battle between the Cuban-American community in Miami and the Cuban government. The U.S. government gave Elián back to his father.

Elián's mother and the other Cubans who tried to immigrate in the 1980s and 1990s were not as wealthy as the earlier arrivals. About ten thousand were criminals. Castro had used the Mariel boat lift to rid his

Famous Immigrant
Gloria Estefan, Singer, Actress
(1957–)

Born in Havana, Cuba, Gloria came to the United States with her family when Fidel Castro took over Cuba in 1959. Her father took part in a failed invasion of Cuba and was imprisoned there for a year and a half. While earning a degree in psychology, Gloria sang with a Latin band, the Miami Sound Machine. She married the band's keyboard player, Emilio Estefan.

Singing in both Spanish and English, Gloria Estefan attracts a wide audience. Dubbed the "Queen of Latin Pop," she has topped the pop, dance, rhythm-and-blues, and Latin charts. Her 1993 album *Mi Tierra* (My Homeland) featured Cuban music of the 1930s and 1940s. She has sold over 45 million records.

Gloria Estefan nearly died in a bus crash in 1990. Doctors had to insert a titanium rod in her back to stabilize her spine. She could not perform for a year.

One of the highlights of her career was performing at the 1996 Olympic Games in Atlanta, Georgia. Another was her first acting experience, in the movie *Music of the Heart,* the true story of a music teacher in Harlem.

Gloria Estefan describes herself as a woman with an American head and a Cuban heart.

country of people he did not want. But by far the majority of the Cubans who settled in Florida were hardworking people. They began businesses, opened banks, and established Cuban-American organizations. They formed Spanish-language newspapers and radio and television stations. They got involved in sports, entertainment, and politics. The Cuban immigrants brought to Miami and the entire country a rich, sophisticated, colorful Latin culture.

Other Latin-American Immigrants

Cubans, Mexicans, and Puerto Ricans were not the only Latin immigrants. Much of South and Central America

Famous Immigrant
Jaime Escalante, Teacher
(1930–)

From a poor South American Indian family in Bolivia, Jaime Escalante rose to become a well-respected physics teacher. Political and economic instability in Bolivia brought him to the United States in 1963.

Because he could not speak English, Escalante began his life in America sweeping floors. He worked his way up to better positions while learning the language. He discovered that to teach in the United States he had to get an American degree. He had to repeat his entire college education. It took him ten years.

For seventeen years, Escalante taught high-school students in the barrios of Los Angeles. Then he taught six years in a working-class school in Sacramento. He took students others had given up on and motivated them to do well. He became famous when his story was told in the movie *Stand and Deliver*. His students had been accused of cheating on an advanced placement calculus exam. When the students took the test over again, they passed with high marks.

Although retired from teaching, Escalante's continued influence lives on in educational programs he founded for inner-city students and a video series, called *Futures*, that shows how science and math are used in real-world careers. He has won many awards.

and the islands of the Caribbean were in serious turmoil during the last half of the twentieth century. Communist rebels were trying to overthrow some governments. Economies were failing. Rulers were harsh. Increasingly, Latin Americans looked north for economic opportunity and freedom from violence.

In the 1960s and 1970s, thousands fled El Salvador, Panama, Guatemala, Nicaragua, and Honduras. In the 1980s, refugees from Haiti came to the United States. More came when the Haitian government was toppled in 1991. Many El Salvadorans immigrated during a civil war that ended in 1992. Many more were driven north by major earthquakes in 2001. In the 1990s, almost three hundred forty thousand people from the Dominican Republic came to the United States.[10]

Most of the Latin-American immigrants settled in ethnic communities. About half are in Texas and California. Mexican Americans and Central Americans tended to live in the Southwest. Cubans and Haitians stayed in the Southeast, mainly Florida. Puerto Ricans and Dominicans lived in New York City. Many hoped to return to their native lands; most could not.

From Many Lands

Although the greatest numbers of immigrants in the late twentieth century were from Asia and North and South America, Europeans also came. Some fled persecution. In 1956, the people of Hungary revolted against their Communist government. The revolt was put down brutally, and thirty-eight thousand

Hungarians fled to the United States.[11] But the National Origins Act allowed very few Eastern Europeans into the country. Still, Americans wanted to help these "huddled masses yearning to breathe free."[12] So Congress passed the Refugee-Escapee Act in 1957. It allowed those facing Communist persecution to bypass the quotas of the National Origins Act. Throughout the 1960s, this legislation helped people flee oppression in Korea, Yugoslavia, China, and other eastern countries.

Throughout the last years of the twentieth century and into the twenty-first, the pace of immigration picked up. Some people were driven by wars, such as

Palestinian-Americans are only a few of the three hundred thousand Arab Americans living in New York City.

the Iraq War of 1990 and a war between the African nations of Eritrea and Ethiopia in 1998. Others fled civil war, such as that in Bosnia in 1992. The chaos that followed the breakup of the Soviet Union in the 1990s brought people from Russia, Afghanistan, and other Eastern European countries.

Some of the recent immigrants are from the Middle East. In 1970, the number of people originally from Middle Eastern countries living in the United States was less than two hundred thousand. By 2000, that figure had jumped to 1.5 million. The majority are from Iran, Pakistan, Israel, and Bangladesh, in that order. Sizeable numbers are from Turkey, Egypt, and Lebanon. Only 15 percent of the Middle Easterners in the United States were Muslim in 1970; in 2000, 73 percent were Muslim. Most came to escape political corruption and oppression and find better economic opportunities.[13]

Whatever their reasons for coming, people from many lands, many ethnic groups, many traditions are welcomed in the United States. That policy was established at the nation's start. President George Washington made that clear when he said, "The bosom of America is open to receive not only the Opulent [wealthy] and respectable Stranger, but the oppressed and persecuted of all Nations and Religions."[14] And in the twenty-first century, America is home to people of nearly every nation and religion on earth.

A Nation of Many Peoples

As early as 1792, a French immigrant called the United States a "melting pot." In America, he said, "individuals of all nations are melted into a new race of men."[1] His idea was that immigrants would shed the habits and thinking of their homelands. They would develop new patterns, dictated by life in their new land. Eventually, all Americans, no matter where they came from, would be very similar. They would not be European, Asian, or African, but "a new race" called American.

The melting pot, however, was always a myth. People generally immigrated together. They stayed in ethnic or national groups. They valued the ways of their native countries. They did not melt together into one new culture. Instead, they blended their different traditions. Rather than a melting pot, America is more like a stew. All the ingredients are distinct, each lending flavor and color to the whole.

This concept is known as multiculturalism or ethnic pluralism. The United States has a plurality—a lot—of ethnic and cultural groups. Everyone does not look and act like everyone else. There is no single image of what it means to be American.

Immigration Concerns

There is no single idea of how to deal with the concerns people have about immigration today. One major concern is illegal immigration. No one knows how many people are in the country illegally, but estimates run over 10 million. People frequently assume that illegal aliens are Mexicans who creep across the southern border at night. Some are. But some are people who walk across the northern border from Canada. Canadians are permitted to travel in the United States for six months without a visa. Therefore, many are not

A family tries to run across the border near Tijuana, Mexico, in 1991.

checked, and some abuse the privilege. These are common pictures people have of illegals. However, 25 to 40 percent of the illegal immigrants are not border crossers. They are visa abusers. They initially came into the country legally. But their visas are temporary. They are student visas, travel visas, work visas, or some other limited document. When the visa expires, the guest is supposed to return home. Every year, thousands, perhaps millions, simply stay. They could be from any nation.[2]

More than 80 percent of illegal immigrants enter the United States across its southern border. Some people want to stop them from coming by building a fence along the border. They want a physical fence in some places and electronic alarm systems in others. Some people want to make coming legally easier. They suggest a guest worker arrangement like the *bracero* program of the 1940s and 1950s. With such a program, fewer would-be immigrants would resort to trying to sneak in.

Congress has tried to deal with the problems of illegal immigration through legislation. The 1986 Immigration Reform and Control Act was one such attempt. It offered amnesty—a pardon—to any undocumented alien who entered the United States before 1982. This made many of the Mexican immigrants who entered the United States without documents legal citizens. The law also forbade employers from hiring illegals. It imposed sanctions on companies that employed undocumented workers.

The 2001 Patriot Act dealt with another problem related to immigrants. This issue arose after the terrorist attacks of 9/11. Some Americans were concerned that if getting into the country illegally was easy, terrorists might have little problem finding their way in. So the Patriot Act plugged up some immigration holes. It called for a more secure visa system. Visa holders could be identified through voiceprints, fingerprints, or some other impossible-to-copy method. It mandated tamper-proof visa documents. The law also required stricter monitoring of student visas. It put more agents on patrol at the borders. In 2003, the Immigration and Naturalization Service became part of the Department of Homeland Security.

Some people have complained that measures such as the Patriot Act restrict too many freedoms. Others argue that the issue of terrorism overrides all other concerns. Some people want open borders. Others want to close the country off to nearly all newcomers. Most agree that when immigration is legal and adequately controlled, it is good for America.

Immigrants Enrich America

Every immigrant group and every individual immigrant has contributed something to America. Every group has left its stamp on the country. That stamp can be seen in the names of cities, rivers, and states. The nation abounds in Latino names, such as Los Angeles, Las Cruces, and San Antonio. The Russian

River and China Lake recall the presence of immigrants in California.

The different peoples that have settled America have left their mark on the language as well. Many of our ranching terms are from the Mexicans who first herded cattle in the West. *Lariat*, *lasso*, and *stampede*, for example, are all from Spanish words. Germans have lent educational terms such as *kindergarten* and *gymnasium*. Italians have given us many musical terms: *soprano*, *aria*, *tempo*, *crescendo*, and *a cappella*. *Chow*, which we use to mean food, is a meat dumpling in China. The Irish have given us the *paddy wagon* and the expression *"take the cake."*

Immigrants brought their art forms to their new country. Mexicans sang ballad-like *corridos*; Cubans danced the rumba and the conga; Germans played tubas in outdoor band performances; Italians introduced opera. African Americans created unique forms of music from their experiences in the United States: gospel, blues, and jazz. The music, art, and literature of many cultures have nourished the American soul.

Many great American inventions were the work of immigrants. The world's largest piano factory was built by German immigrant Henry Steinway. The first American optical company was founded by Germans John Bausch and Henry Lomb. Alexander Graham Bell, who invented the telephone, was from Scotland. The Saturn V rocket that took the first men to the moon was the work of German immigrant Wernher von Braun. Italian immigrant Enrico Fermi's scientific research led to the atomic bomb. The research of German immigrant Albert Einstein was world famous. Hungarian Edward Teller's scientific theories were very influential. Blue jeans, hamburgers, and ketchup—all were created in America by immigrants.

Much that is now called American was begun by immigrants. The Uncle Sam figure that represents the United States all over the world was designed by German immigrant Thomas Nast. He also created the Democratic donkey and the Republican elephant. Chinese immigrant I. M. Pei was the architect for

Uncle Sam was designed by German immigrant Thomas Nast. Nast also drew political cartoons for American newspapers.

America's National Gallery of Art. The institution that is today the Bank of America was begun as the Bank of Italy by immigrant A. P. Giannini. The song "God Bless America" was written by a grateful Russian immigrant, Irving Berlin. Even the name "America" is not native. It is from Italian sailor Amerigo Vespucci.

The influence of immigrants can be seen in festive events all across the country. St. Patrick's Day parades. Swedish, Greek, and Scottish festivals. Octoberfests, Hmong New Year, Cinco de Mayo, and the dozens of Italian feast days. These are not foreign customs brought to America's shores. They have become American traditions, enjoyed by recent immigrants and "native" Americans alike.

These contributions are only the more obvious of the gifts immigrants brought to the United States. More importantly, they brought a hunger for freedom. And they brought a determination to work hard and achieve. Every immigrant reminded Americans, the children of immigrants, of the liberty and opportunities they have. As President John F. Kennedy said, "Every ethnic minority, in seeking its own freedom, helped strengthen the fabric of liberty in American life."[3]

That fabric remains strong because people continue to come. In the 1990s, more than 8.5 million immigrants were admitted to the United States.[4] This was more than in any previous decade. The present time may become the new century of immigration.

The differences that so many people from so many places bring are obvious. In the New York borough of

Over 280 people from 67 countries were sworn in as U.S. citizens at the Eleventh Annual Fiesta of Independence at South Mountain Community College in Phoenix, Arizona in 2003.

Queens, 138 languages are spoken.[5] In Los Angeles County, at least 224 languages can be heard.[6] In many malls, shoppers can choose from Greek, Armenian, Mexican, Japanese, Indian, and Thai restaurants or a host of others. These differences are part of the richness of America. They are the reasons for its greatness. President Lyndon Johnson once remarked, "America . . . flourished because it was fed from so many sources— because it was nourished by so many cultures and traditions and peoples."[7]

No other country is made up of so many cultures and peoples. No other nation receives people from so many different places. America is unique among the nations of the world because it is a nation of immigrants.

1607 First British colony in America founded at Jamestown, Virginia.

1619–1808 Slave trade brings black men, women, and children from Africa.

1845–1848 Potato Famine in Ireland sparks immigration.

1848 Revolution in Germany sparks immigration. At end of Mexican-American War, United States acquires land from Mexico. Thousand of Mexicans now find themselves Americans.

1849 California gold rush sparks immigration from China.

1868 Japanese come to Hawaii to work in sugarcane fields.

1875 Federal government rather than state governments placed in charge of immigration.

1880–1910 Economic and political troubles spark immigration from Italy, Greece, and countries of eastern Europe.

1882 Laws in Russia intensify pressure on Jews, sparking immigration. Chinese Exclusion Act makes immigration from China illegal.

1892–1954 U.S. immigration station on Ellis Island in New York Harbor processes immigrants.

1907–1908 Gentleman's agreement between United States and Japan.

1910–1940 Angel Island immigration station operates in California.

1911 Mexican revolution sparks immigration.

1917–1924 Series of laws restrict immigration.

1924 National Origins Act establishes quota system.

1942–1964 *Bracero* program allows Mexicans to enter United States as temporary workers.

1943 Congress repeals Chinese Exclusion Law.

1948 Displaced Persons Act allows people displaced from their homes in World War II to immigrate.

1953 Refugee Relief Act permits certain refugees from war-torn countries to bypass quota system.

1956 Repression of revolt in Hungary sparks immigration.

1957 Refugee-Escapee Act allows those facing Communist persecution to bypass quotas.

1959 Fidel Castro's revolution in Cuba sparks immigration from Cuba.

1965 Immigration Act repeals system of quotas based on national origin.

1975 End of war in Vietnam sparks immigration from Southeast Asia.

1980 Mariel Harbor boat lift brings Cuban refugees to Florida. Refugee Act establishes general policy governing admission of refugees.

1986 Immigration Reform and Control Act legalizes hundreds of thousands of illegal immigrants.

1990s Political and economic strife in Latin American, African, Middle Eastern, and some European countries spark immigration. Changes in the former Soviet Union spark immigration.

2001 USA Patriot Act attempts to tighten immigration controls.

2003 The Immigration and Naturalization Service becomes part of the Department of Homeland Security.

Escape From Germany

1. Kurt Burger in a letter to his son, excerpted in Bernard A. Weisberger, *The American Heritage History of the American People* (New York: American Heritage, 1971), pp. 336–337.

Chapter One   Settling America

1. Elaine Dewar, *Bones: Discovering the First Americans* (New York: Carroll & Graf, 2002); William Fitzhugh, Ives Goddard, Steve Ousley, Doug Ousley, and Dennis Stanford, *Paleoamerican Origins*, Smithsonian Institution, 1999, <http://www.si.edu/resource/faq/nmnh/origin.htm> (December 2, 2005).

2. Portugal established a colony in Brazil before Spain founded a colony, but Portugal did not have a colony in the territory that would become the United States.

3. From the Bible, Matthew 5:14: "Ye are the light of the world. A city that is set on an hill cannot be hid."

4. J. C. Furnas, *The Americans: A Social History of the United States 1587–1914* (New York: Putnam, 1969), p. 58.

5. Ibid., p. 73.

6. Samuel Eliot Morison, *Oxford History of the American People* (New York: Oxford University Press, 1965), p. 77.

7. Philip Curtin, *The Atlantic Slave Trade: A Census* (Madison: University of Wisconsin Press, 1969), pp. 87–88.

8. Richard Hofstadter, *America at 1750: A Social Portrait* (New York: Vintage, 1973), p. 89.

9. Kenneth Finkel, "Marking Pennsylvania History," *WHYY*, n.d., <http://www.whyy.org/91FM/marker_purchase.html> (December 2, 2005).

10. Roger Daniels, *Coming to America: A History of Immigration and Ethnicity in American Life,* 2nd edition (New York: Perennial, 2002), pp. 34–41.

Chapter Two Growing America

1. Richard Hofstadter, *America at 1750: A Social Portrait* (New York: Vintage, 1973), p. 5.

2. Russel Blaine Nye, *Society and Culture in America, 1830–1860* (New York: Harper and Row, 1974), p. 202.

3. Ibid.

4. Roger Daniels, *Coming to America: A History of Immigration and Ethnicity in American Life*, 2nd edition (New York: Perennial, 2002), p. 129, reported that Irish comprised 45.6 percent of total immigration in the 1840s.

5. Library of Congress, *Immigration: Irish,* April 6, 2002, <http://memory.loc.gov/learn/features/immig/irish2.html> (November 22, 2004).

6. Ronald Takaki, *A Different Mirror: A History of Multicultural America* (Boston: Little, Brown, and Company, 1993), p. 144.

7. Nye, p. 204.

8. Bernard A. Weisberger, *The American Heritage History of the American People* (New York: American Heritage, 1971), p. 113.

9. L. H. Gann and Peter J. Duignan, *The Hispanics*

in the United States: A History (Boulder, Colo.: Westview Press, 1986), p. 18.

10. Ibid., p. 20.

11. Weisberger, p. 217.

12. Daniels, pp. 124–125.

13. U.S. Immigration and Naturalization Service, *Statistical Yearbook of the Immigration and Naturalization Service, 2000* (Washington, D.C: U.S. Government Printing Office, 2002), Table 2.

Chapter Three   Building America

1. James M. Jasper, *Restless Nation: Starting Over in America* (Chicago: University of Chicago, 2000), p. 66.

2. Roger Daniels, *Coming to America: A History of Immigration and Ethnicity in American Life,* 2nd edition (New York: Perennial, 2002), p. 130.

3. "Years of Growth: 1835–1860," *National Railroad Museum* 2005, <http://www.national rrmuseum.org/collections-exhibits/outline/years-of-growth.php> (February 11, 2005).

4. Ronald Takaki, *A Different Mirror: A History of Multicultural America* (Boston: Little, Brown, and Company, 1993), p. 197.

5. Samuel Eliot Morison, *Oxford History of the American People* (New York: Oxford University Press, 1965), p. 669.

6. Bernard A. Weisberger, *The American Heritage History of the American People* (New York: American Heritage, 1971), p. 220.

Chapter Four   Defining America

1. Alan Brinkley, *American History: A Survey,* vol. 2 (New York: McGraw-Hill, 1995), p. 509.

2. "History of Ellis Island," *Ellis Island,* n.d., <http://www.ellisislandimmigrants.org/ellis_island_history.htm> (March 11, 2005).

3. "The Detained Immigrant," *Harper's Weekly,* August 26, 1893, reprinted in <http://www.for-tunecity.com/littleitaly/amalfi/100/deten93.htm> (March 11, 2005).

4. "History of Ellis Island."

5. U.S. Immigration and Naturalization Service, *Statistical Yearbook of the Immigration and Naturalization Service, 2000* (Washington, D.C: U.S. Government Printing Office, 2002), Table 2.

6. Library of Congress, *Immigration: Polish/Russian,* August 9, 2004, <http://memory.loc.gov/learn/features/immig/polish5.html> (October 11, 2004).

7. Ronald Takaki, *A Different Mirror: A History of Multicultural America* (Boston: Little, Brown, and Company, 1993), p. 248.

8. Roger Daniels, *Coming to America: A History of Immigration and Ethnicity in American Life,* 2nd edition (New York: Perennial, 2002), pp. 258–259.

9. Bernard A. Weisberger, *The American Heritage History of the American People* (New York: American Heritage, 1971), p. 350.

10. U.S. Immigration and Naturalization Service, Table 2.

11. Library of Congress, *Immigration: Mexican,* September 11, 2003, <http://memory.loc.gov/learn/

features/immig/mexican4.html> (October 10, 2004).

12. Brinkley, p. 546.

Chapter Five   America Restricts Immigration

1. Library of Congress, *Immigration: Chinese,* September 1, 2003, <http://memory.loc.gov/learn/ features/immig/chinese9.html> (November 22, 2004).

2. Library of Congress, *Immigration: Japanese,* February 2, 2004, <http://memory.loc.gov/learn/ features/immig/japanese4.html> (November 22, 2004).

3. Ibid.

Chapter Six   Immigration Slows

1. Roger Daniels, *Coming to America: A History of Immigration and Ethnicity in American Life,* 2nd edition (New York: Perennial, 2002), pp. 294–295.

2. Library of Congress, *Immigration: Mexican,* September 11, 2003, <http://memory.loc.gov/learn/ features/immig/mexican8.html> (October 10, 2004).

3. Ibid.

4. Daniels, p. 300.

5. U.S. Immigration and Naturalization Service, *Statistical Yearbook of the Immigration and Naturalization Service, 2000* (Washington, D.C: U.S. Government Printing Office, 2002), Table 2.

6. "Immigration Station," *Angel Island* 1998–2003, <http://www.angelisland.org/immigr02.html> October 23, 2004.

7. Ibid.

8. U.S. Immigration and Naturalization Service, Table 2.

Chapter Seven   Changing Patterns of Immigration

1. Reshmi Hebbar, "Filipino American Literature," *Emory University*, Spring 1998, <http://www. english.emory.edu/Bahri/Filipino.html> (November 1, 2005).

2. Roger Daniels, *Guarding the Golden Door: American Immigration Policy and Immigrants Since 1882* (New York: Hill and Wang, 2004), p. 216.

3. Jennifer Yau, "The Foreign-Born Hmong in the United States," *Migration Information Source,* January 1, 2005, <http://www.migrationinformation. org/USFocus/display.cfm?ID=281> (March 22, 2005).

4. L. H. Gann and Peter J. Duignan, *The Hispanics in the United States: A History* (Boulder, Colo.: Westview Press, 1986), pp. 150–151.

5. Ibid., p. 160.

6. Library of Congress, *Immigration: Puerto Rican/ Cuban,* April 22, 2004, <http://memory.loc.gov/ learn/features/immig/cuban3.html> (October 7, 2004).

7. Bernard A. Weisberger, *The American Heritage History of the American People* (New York: American Heritage, 1971), p. 359.

8. Library of Congress, *Immigration: Puerto Rican/ Cuban.*

9. Judy L. Silverstein, "Memories of Mariel: Twenty Years Later," *U.S. Coast Guard Reserve Magazine*, April 2000 [on-line], <http://www.uscg.mil/reserve/magazine/mag2000/apr2000/mariel.htm> (October 7, 2004).

10. Elizabeth Grieco, "The Foreign Born from the Dominican Republic in the United States," *Migration Information Source*, October 1, 2004, <http://www.migrationinformation.org/Usfocus/display.cfm?id=259> (March 21, 2005).

11. Federation for American Immigration Reform, *U.S. Immigration History*, July 2004, <http://www.fairus.org/Research/Research.cfm?ID=1820&c=2> (October 4, 2004).

12. From Emma Lazarus's poem engraved on the pedestal of the Statue of Liberty.

13. Steven A. Camarota, "Immigrants from the Middle East: A Profile of the Foreign-born Population from Pakistan to Morocco," *Center for Immigration Studies*, August 2002, <http://www.cis.org/articles/2002/back902.html> (November 3, 2005).

14. George Washington, "George Washington to the Members of the Volunteer Association and Other Inhabitants of the Kingdom of Ireland Who Have Lately Arrived in the City of New York," *The Writings of George Washington*, ed. John C. Fitzpatrick (Washington, D.C: U.S. Government Printing Office, 1938), 27, pp. 253–254.

Chapter Eight   A Nation of Many Peoples
1. J. Hector St. John de Crèvecoeur, *Letters From an*

American Farmer (London: Thomas Davies, 1782; reprint, New York: E. P. Dutton, 1957), p. 34.

2. Roger Daniels, *Coming to America: A History of Immigration and Ethnicity in American Life*, 2nd edition (New York: Perennial, 2002), pp. 311, 401, 420–21.

3. John F. Kennedy, *A Nation of Immigrants*, Revised and Enlarged Edition (New York: Harper and Row, 1964), p. 65.

4. Andrew Batchelor, "Executive Summary: U.S. Immigration: A Legislative History," *Population Resource Center*, December 2004, <http://www.prcdc.org/summaries/usimmighistory/usimmig history.html> (December 27, 2004).

5. H. Carl McCall, *Queens: An Economic Review* (report 11-2000) (New York: Office of the State Deputy Comptroller for the City of New York, January 2000), Executive Summary.

6. "Language Spoken at Home by Individual Los Angeles Communities, *Los Angeles Almanac*, 2005, <http://www.LAAlmanac.com/LA/la10b.htm> (March 27, 2005).

7. Lyndon B. Johnson, "Remarks on Immigration Law," *Congressional Quarterly 23*, October 1965, pp. 2063–2064.

amnesty—Official pardon for a crime.

assimilate—To become like people in the dominant culture so as to be unrecognized as different from that culture; to be absorbed into the larger society.

barrio—Area of a city inhabited almost exclusively by Spanish-speaking people.

bracero—Mexican citizen who worked in the United States under contract, as a "guest worker."

coyote—Person who smuggles people from Mexico into the United States.

ethnic pluralism—Concept of a society in which people of different ethnic backgrounds preserve their distinctive cultural identities.

exile—A person forced to leave his native country.

ghetto—Area of a city inhabited almost exclusively by people from an ethnic or national group.

head-right—Land distribution system common in the early colonies. A governor granted land to a person who brought colonists and paid the governor rent on the land.

isolationist—Desire to be free from political and economic ties to foreign countries.

multiculturalism—Movement toward ethnic pluralism in the 1980s and 1990s.

nativist—Person who favors native-born citizens over foreign-born citizens.

naturalization—Process by which a foreign-born person becomes a citizen.

patroon—Men from the Netherlands who brought at least fifty colonists to the New World. They were given estates in the New World in return.

quota—A certain number, usually based on a percentage or other proportion.

steerage—Part of a passenger ship that is below the top deck and assigned to the lowest-paying passengers.

tenement—Building with rooms that are rented out to several families. Tenements are often poor quality buildings located in poor areas.

visa—Document issued to a foreigner coming to the United States that indicates and approves the foreigner's intentions in coming to the United States.

Aldridge, Rebecca. *Italian Americans*. Northborough, Mass.: Chelsea House, 2003.

Bloom, Barbara Lee. *Mexican Americans*. San Diego, Calif.: Lucent, 2003.

Conley, Kate A. *Puerto Rican Americans*. Farmington Hills, Mich.: Thomson Gale, 2005.

Frost, Helen. *Russian Immigrants*, 1860–1915. Mankato, Minn.: Capstone Press, 2002.

Girod, Christina M., and Scott Ingram. *Indian Americans*. Farmington Hills, Mich.: Gale Group, 2003.

Granfield, Linda, and Arlene Alda. *97 Orchard Street, New York: Stories of Immigrant Life*. Toronto, Canada: Tundra, 2001.

Graves, Karry A. *Irish Americans*. Northborough, Mass.: Chelsea House, 2003.

Greene, Meg. *Greek Americans*. San Diego, Calif.: Lucent, 2003.

———. *Polish Americans*. San Diego, Calif.: Lucent, 2003.

Martin, Michael. *Chinese Americans*. Northborough, Mass.: Chelsea House, 2003.

Sonneborn, Liz. *German Americans*. Northborough, Mass.: Chelsea House, 2003.

Zurlo, Tony. *Japanese Americans*. Farmington Hills, Mich.: Thomson Gale, 2003.

History of Angel Island Immigration Station
<http://www.angelisland.org/>
Click on "Immigration Stn" on the right.

History of Ellis Island
<http://www.ellisisland.org/>
Click "Enter."

Library of Congress Information on Historic Information in General and by Specific Group Immigration:
<http://memory.loc.gov>
Click on "Teachers." Select "Features and Activities." Scroll down and click on "Immigration."